The Golf Dictionary

A GUIDE TO THE LANGUAGE AND LINGO OF THE GAME

The Golf Dictionary

A GUIDE TO THE LANGUAGE
AND LINGO OF THE GAME

Michael Corcoran
A Mountain Lion Book

Taylor Publishing Company
Dallas, Texas

Copyright © 1997 by Mountain Lion, Inc.

Published by Taylor Publishing Company
1550 West Mockingbird Lane
Dallas, Texas 75235

Designed by Hespenheide Design

Library of Congress Cataloging-in-Publication Data

Corcoran, Michael.
      The golf dictionary : a guide to the language and lingo of
the game / Michael Corcoran.
          p.   cm.
      ISBN 0-87833-951-5
      1. Golf—Dictionaries.   2. Golf—Terminology.   I. Title.
GV965.C663   1997
      796.352'03—dc21   96-54061
                                                   CIP

Printed in the United States of America
10   9   8   7   6   5   4   3   2   1

About the Author

Michael Corcoran is a former editor in chief of *Golf Illustrated* and *Petersen's Golfing*. During his time as editor of *Golf Illustrated*, the magazine was nominated for general excellence in the area of sports, recreation, and outdoor magazines by the Western Publishing Association. He has written about golf for most of the major consumer and trade magazines and was the managing editor of the *Wide World of Golf* video series, as well as writer for the videos *Scramble to Better Golf with Fuzzy Zoeller* and *The Total Putting Guide with Bob Rosburg*.

Corcoran is currently the executive editor of *Men's Health Daily* at Rodale Press (www.menshealth.com). He lives with his wife and their three children in Ottsville, Pennsylvania.

Acknowledgments

Most of the real work on this book was done by my best friend, Angela Corcoran, who also happens to be my wife. She patiently waded through volumes of correspondence and spent countless hours in front of the computer, entering items from the mounds of lists we compiled. She also put up with my temper tantrums and foul moods as the work piled up. She didn't have to do any of it. But she did.

This book was the brainchild of Randy Voorhees of Mountain Lion, Incorporated. I'm honored that he asked me to write it. In the process, we've become good friends. He even took our kids fishing one day. Now

that's a friend. I'd also like to thank Randy's boss, John Monteleone, the president of Mountain Lion, for giving me the chance to work on this book.

In the course of my time as a golf writer and editor, I've made a lot of friends, but none as special as Joe Passov. If you're a golf fan, you've probably read and enjoyed his work under his full name, Joseph Mark Passov. Joepa, as I prefer to call him, knows more about golf than any living person, and more than a few dead people, too. He was kind enough to endure many hours on the telephone, listening to me query him about various portions of this book, and did so with a lot of laughs and a lot of earnest interest. Guys like Joe Passov don't come around the corner every day, and I'm damned happy he came around my corner a few years back when we worked together in Phoenix. I look forward to the day when I can help him with his first book.

The following people all graciously contributed their time and thoughts to this book by reviewing lists and making suggestions: Jim Apfelbaum, of Austin, Texas, a fine writer and student of the game; Archie Baird, of East Lothian, Scotland, one of the most knowledgeable golf people in the world and author of *Golf on Guillane Hill*; Rich Bernstein, of Kendall Park, New Jersey, a true golf nut and great guy; Robert Boland Jr., Warrington, Pennsylvania, an old friend of the Corcoran family and, just as important, a former Old York Road caddie; Jack Bonner, Myrtle Beach, South Carolina, another family friend and actually my high school golf coach for a few weeks; Jeff Fair, Coopersburg, Pennsylvania; Jules Furth, Chicago, Illinois; David Gould, Sandy Hook, Connecticut, once my editor and the single finest writer of golf prose I've ever had the pleasure to read; Dan Gleason, Woodstock, Georgia, a good friend and very funny writer; Russ Jimeson, Grand Rapids, Michigan; John Bateman, Warrington, Pennsylvania, who has stood by me through thick and thin; Lori Kavanaugh, Tucson, Arizona, Joepa's sister, who is married to the very talented course architect Ken Kavanaugh; Edward Kipe, Plymouth Meeting, Pennsylvania, one of the many fine members of the Old York Road Country Club for whom I caddied as a boy; Bradley Klein, Bloomfield, Connecticut, a noted golf historian and architecture expert; John Ledesma, Los Angeles, California, a smart, young guy with a huge future ahead of him (he's the managing editor of *Golf Tips* magazine); Lyn Peightal, Edgewater, Florida, an Internet buddy who is fun to talk with; John Poinier, Phoenix, Arizona, one of my mates from my days at *Golf Illustrated* and one of the brightest people I've ever known; Ian Scott, Surrey, England, father of one of my dearest friends, Elaine Scott, the director of communications for the LPGA; John Hopkins, London, England, golf and rugby writer for the *Times* in London and someone I'd like to be when I grow up; the Brothers Corcoran—Thomas, Timothy, James, and Philip—who all contributed to this book and to my formative understanding of the game;

Thomas and Mary Corcoran, my parents, whom I love more than I've ever been able to tell them.

Finally, three of my colleagues from Rodale Press have been very helpful to me in the latter stages of this book. Jordan Matus, who works with me at *Men's Health Daily*, and Mark Remy, an editor at *Men's Health* magazine, did some yeomanlike copyediting. Jennifer Haigh, also an editor at *Men's Health* magazine, read and commented on parts of this book.

Thank you all, very much.

Introduction

If you love golf, nothing is quite like the sound of a golf course coming to life in the morning. I learned about this early in life as a caddie at Old York Road Country Club in Spring House, Pennsylvania, just a short drive outside the city limits of Philadelphia. From the time I was eleven until I was well into my early twenties, I spent my weekend mornings sitting around the yard in front of the caddyshack, listening to the stories of the bards of the yard. Most of the stories involved their loops from the previous day or things that had happened years before at the club. Every golf club has its infamous stories, and no one tells them better than the caddies. I loved those mornings in the yard, nursing a cup of hot coffee and, when I got a little older, the occasional hangover. I was more of a listener than a spinner.

My appreciation for the game of golf was born during those years, as was a fondness for the language of the game. A caddie was a *looper* and a great caddie was a *super looper*. A caddie who had been at the club a long time was a *toad* (a term not in this book because I have never heard it used anywhere else). Old York Road was the place I learned the meaning of fat and thin, skinny and chunky, chili-dip and pure.

This book is not a reference book or an authoritative book on golf history, the Rules of Golf, or the golf swing, although all of those things are mentioned. Rather, it was written with the intent of shedding a little practical light on the everyday language of the game of golf. After years of writing about the game, I realized that not all golfers, even enthusiastic ones, knew how to speak like real golfers, and most frequently misunderstood a lot of the jargon, particularly as it related to the swing. This book is an attempt to help you enjoy the lingo of the game and to make sure you know what the hell someone means when they talk about *casting from the top* or *too much right hand*.

You will undoubtedly notice that this book touches on some elements of the Rules of Golf, that it lists the names of some golfers, some golf courses, and some of the noted landmarks on golf courses. Why is some stuff in this book and other stuff not?

First, some terms in this book are obsolete, but are occasionally still used or are neat enough that you might enjoy using them. Some obsolete terms were left out because you really wouldn't have an opportunity to use them, nor would you probably care to. Such a word is *sinker*, which referred to a ball that would sink when it landed in the water. *Sinker* isn't in the book, but *foozle* is because it's a fun word.

There are some terms that relate to the Rules of Golf, but the rules are boring and voluminous, so no attempt was made to thoroughly present them. What you will find in this book relating to the rules are some practical usages you should know in case you ever get in a bar conversation with a bore.

There are some golfers mentioned in this book, too. Why is Johnny Miller included and Raymond Floyd not? After all, Floyd has won more major championships than Miller. The criteria for the inclusion of players in this book was the following: If a golfer from another planet showed up in the grillroom and sat at your table, wanting to know about some famous golfers, which ones would you mention? You would want to mention Miller because he ruled the game for a few years in the early 1970s and played the greatest final round ever in the U.S. Open. Raymond Floyd, for all of his accomplishments, wouldn't interest a visitor from another planet. Miller, with his charisma and startling scoring ability, would. For the same reason, Jan Stephenson is in the book, and Patty Sheehan is not.

What about golf courses? That's a book unto itself, so this book includes ten golf courses that our friend from another world would need to know about if he were to talk Earth-golf with his pals back home. The courses were chosen based on history and the impact their existence has had on the game. Some neat golf course landmarks are also included, such as the Valley of Sin, simply because they have a nice ring to them.

A few more notes: There's a lot in this book on the golf swing. Everything on this subject is written as it would apply to a right-handed golfer since the majority of golfers play right-handed. Sorry about that if you're a lefty, but it makes for clumsy writing. Also, the pronouns in this book are all masculine. I realize that more and more women are playing golf every day, but the "he/she" business also makes for clumsy writing, and writing it in a neutral manner was out of the question based on the voice the book was meant to convey. My apologies to anyone offended by this.

Finally, one notable non-entry in this book is the word *golf*. That could have made for a chapter in itself, and there is no consensus on the origin and meaning of the word. It's a safe assumption that you know what golf means to you, and that's all that matters. If you're not convinced that's a good enough reason, read the following from Dan Jenkins's *Dogged Victims of Inexorable Fate*, a book you really should read if you already haven't. "Some," writes Jenkins pretending to be an ancient Scot, "say the Romans did it [invent golf] long before me and called it *Pagancia*, which I think, between you and me, sounds like a joint over on East 56th with a big tab. Some say the Dutch invented golf, or a game called *kolven*, which was similar. But no way. *Kolven* has to be a roll of veal stuffed with cheese and chives. Some say that even the French originated golf under the name of *jeu de mail*, but as any European traveler knows, this is a card game for the big players in Monaco. Actually, if the historians want to be picky, you could say that the Chinese a thousand years ago probably played a form of golf by batting a few snow peas around with chopsticks."

That's all you need to know. Hope you like the book.

ace A hole in one. Since a hole in one is the best of all possible shots in golf, this term probably evolved from the ace in a deck of cards. The ace in cards is the best card and, in certain games, also has a value of one point.

The game has many legends surrounding aces made by famous players. Perhaps the best is the case of J. Wood Platt, a fine amateur player from Philadelphia. Playing a round at Pine Valley, generally regarded as the finest course in the world, Platt birdied the first hole, eagled the second, and *aced* the third, a medium-length par three. After making birdie at the fourth, a difficult par four, Platt stopped in the clubhouse to brace himself before playing the 226-yard, par-three fifth hole, ranked among the sternest par threes in the world. Platt never emerged from the clubhouse. The story goes that he determined there wasn't any point in continuing on.

action If a ball spins backward or bites (see *bite*) once it hits the green, you might say it a had *action* on it. Also, all bets made on a match are collectively known as *action*. If you want to ask someone if they wish to place a small wager on a match, you might say, "You feel like a little action?" For some reason, *action* in betting parlance is almost always preceded by the word *little*.

It is also common to refer to a player's swing as his action, i.e., "He has a nice *action*," to indicate he has a good swing.

address The position that a player takes while preparing to play a shot. The *address* position is the foundation of the golf swing because it is at this moment during the pre-swing preparation process that the player finalizes his aim at the target and sets his body in position to begin the swinging motion.

The term *address* also refers to the act of assuming this position. In this sense, the term plays an important role in determining whether or not a penalty is assessed when the ball moves while a player prepares to play a shot. A penalty is only assessed when the player is deemed to have addressed the ball, and under the Rules of Golf, a player is only deemed to have done so when he has taken his stance (set his feet in position to play the shot) and grounded his club. (In a hazard, a player has addressed the ball once he has taken his stance. This is because it is illegal to ground the club in a hazard.) For this reason, many top level players (Jack Nicklaus and Greg Norman, for exam-ple) do not ground their clubs as they prepare to play a shot. Nicklaus takes this to the extreme by not even grounding his putter as he sets up to putt.

advice If you want advice on your golf game, you should write to Dear Abby because it's against the Rules of Golf for you to ask your opponent or fellow competitor for advice during the course of a round. You may, within the rules, ask your caddie (or partner in team competition) for advice regarding which way the green breaks, the wind blows, or the fairway is slanted—or anything else related to the game.

Here's an odd twist to the practical use of the term *advice*, however: While it is illegal for you to ask your opponent what club he intends to use or has just used, it is within the Rules of Golf for you to look in his bag to see which club he has selected or has just hit. But it gets even better. A good caddie will, of course, cover the clubs with a towel to prevent an opponent from determining the club his man has played. In such a case, it is perfectly legal for the inquisitor to move the towel aside to gain full view of the clubs. Seems like it would be a lot easier to make it legal to ask, don't you think?

aerated For the purposes of maintaining a course's greens and fairways, they are sometimes *aerated*, or have holes roughly the circumference of a nickel punched into the them. When you play a lousy round on a course with aerated greens, it makes for the perfect excuse. Everyone else will just nod and agree when you say, "I couldn't get a single putt to fall, but what can you expect on aerated greens."

afraid of the dark When putt after putt comes close to the hole but won't fall in, you can amuse the lads by saying, "That ball must be *afraid of the dark*." It doesn't make sense actually, since it's no darker in the hole than it is anywhere else, but everyone will get your drift.

A game When you're playing and thinking at the highest level possible for you, you're playing your *A game*. The term is typically used in anticipation of a round yet to be played. If you're playing a course you've never played before and someone says to you, "You better bring your A game," they mean you'll need to play well to handle the course. Likewise, a player who needs to play well in the final round of a tournament might say, "I'll need to bring my A game tomorrow."

It also works well as an excuse for a bad round, i.e., "What can I say? I just didn't have my A game today."

aggregate With the exception of a member-guest tournament, you won't need to use this term too often. An *aggregate* score in medal play (see *medal play*) is the total score for all the rounds played in a given tournament, following the most recently completed round. For example, if you shot 76 in the first round of a tourney and 82 in the second, your aggregate score after two rounds would be 158. You would add your third-round score to this number to determine your three-round aggregate.

Many member-guest tournaments are played in match play format with the winners of a given flight being determined by their aggregate match-play total within the flight. For example, if a team plays five matches within its flight, its match play aggregate is determined by adding up its margins of victory/defeat. So if a team wins its first match one up, its second match one up, and loses its third match one down, the team aggregate is one up heading into the fourth match.

air mail If your shot unintentionally flies over the green, without even

3

touching a little bit of the back of the green, you *air mailed* the green, pal.

air press In golf betting parlance, a press indicates that the trailing player or side wishes to establish a new match within the match, typically beginning from the point when a side is two down and running through the remainder of the match. An *air press* is a bet on a single hole, which can be made by either player while his opponent's ball is in the air on any shot. The air press doubles the value of the hole, and there is no limit on the number of air presses that can be declared on a given hole. The idea, of course, is to press when it appears your opponent's ball is heading for trouble. But you have to call the press before the ball hits the ground.

air shot This is an obsolete term for a whiff, a complete miss. Chances are excellent that you're playing with Bernard Darwin or P. G. Wodehouse if someone in your foursome compliments you on your *air shot*. In fact, it's doubtful even those two gentlemen would compliment you on such an attempted shot.

albatross A score of three under par on a given hole, also called a double eagle (see *double eagle*). The most famous *albatross* in the history of the game was recorded by Gene Sarazen in the second Masters Tournament (1935) when he holed out his second shot at Augusta National's fifteenth hole on his way to winning the event. Sarazen's shot is referred to in the history books as "The Shot Heard 'round the World," a play on the phrase that refers to the opening volley fired in the American Revolution.

UPI/CORBIS-BETTMANN

Gene Sarazen, famed for his albatross at the 1935 Masters.

alignment This refers to act of aiming your body and the clubface at address (see *address*). Specifically, *alignment* refers to the aiming of the clubface, your feet, knees, hips, and shoulders.

all-around *All-around* refers to the overall balance of a player's game. A player who is strong in every phase of the game is said to be a good *all-around* player.

all-exempt tour This refers to the fact that on the modern PGA Tour, players are exempt from qualifying for tournament play from week to week based on a long list of criteria. The criterion that qualifies the largest number of players is the previous year's money list (see *money list*).

all square Originally used only in match play, *all square* referred to a tie at any given point during a match. Today, it is frequently used by commentators to describe a tie between the leaders in medal (stroke) play.

amateur In its strict sense, this term refers to a player who does not accept money for playing in tournaments. To compete in *amateur* competition, however, a modern golfer must adhere to a seemingly endless list of requirements to qualify.

In the early days of golf, when professionals were viewed as old chewing gum on the bottom of golf's collective shoe, amateurs were considered the true "gentlemen" golfers, and amateur-only competitions were considered more important and significant than open competitions that allowed any golfer, including professionals, to participate.

Amateur, the Short for *U.S. Amateur*, the national championship for amateur golfers and the most coveted title in all of amateur golf. Originally, it was considered one of golf's four major championships, along with the British Amateur and the U.S. and British Opens. Today, its status as a major is clouded. The reason for this is that Jack Nicklaus, the greatest competitive golfer of all time, counts his two U.S. Amateur titles in his total of twenty major championships (six Masters, five PGA Championships, four U.S. Opens, three British Opens, and two U.S. Amateurs), as do the history books. The fact is that the Amateur had ceased to be considered a major long before Nicklaus's two victories in it (1959, 1961). The precedent of this tournament as a major dates to the early days of the competition, particularly to the success of the greatest of all amateurs, Bobby Jones, whose five U.S. Amateur titles (from 1924 to 1929) are numbered among his fourteen major titles, placing him second all-time in total majors behind Nicklaus.

amateur side Term for a putt that misses on the low side of the hole (low side depends upon the direction of the break). The term refers to the fact that professional golfers allegedly miss most putts on the high side of the hole because a putt on the low side has little chance of catching any part of the hole and dropping in.

Amen Corner Collectively, the eleventh, twelfth, and thirteenth holes at Augusta National Golf Club, a par four, par three, and par five respectively. It was so christened by the writer Herbert Warren Wind for the fact that a player who survives this stretch of holes without calamity should be thankful. *Amen Corner* is almost certain to be the place where a golfer in contention to win the Masters either stakes his claim to the title or wilts under the pressure of Sunday afternoon.

American ball An outdated term that referred to the ball sanctioned by the United States Golf Association (USGA), which differed from that sanctioned by the Royal and Ancient Golf Club of St. Andrews (R & A) prior to the early 1970s. The *American ball* was specified by the USGA as having a diameter not less than 1.68 inches and a weight not more than 1.62 ounces, while the ball sanctioned by the R & A (commonly referred to in America as the *small ball*) had a slightly smaller diameter and weight. The R & A eventually adopted the American ball as its standard. During the two-ball era, one of the interesting twists of the British Open each year was the question of how American players would adapt to playing the small ball. It was never much of a problem for America's best, who dominated the Open when the small ball was in use.

amphitheater As used in golf, this term refers to a green which sits in a bowl or horseshoe-shaped hollow, allowing spectators a clear view of the proceedings. In modern lingo, this is referred to as stadium golf. Although some courses, such as Augusta National, are considered natural *amphitheaters*, stadium courses are constructed with the express purpose of maximizing the spectators' viewing enjoyment all over the course, not just around the greens.

angle of approach There are two angles of approach to consider in golf. The first is the *angle* at which you bring the clubhead down toward the ball. The second is the *angle* from which you approach the green. There is no variance in the angle of approach on most par threes unless there are multiple tees along multiple lines to the green.

A player, B player, etc. In some club level tournaments, teams are made up by grouping players of varying skill levels. Typically, the best player on a team is the *A player*, the next best player is the *B player*, and so on.

approach Broadly speaking, the *approach* is the area of a given hole that leads up to the green as dictated by the routing and design of the hole. If that sounds vague, it's because it is—no fixed yardage can be set as to when the approach to a green begins or ends. In general, the approach would begin at the point where the player's drive comes to rest (assuming the player hits a drive that is of sufficient distance and accuracy to be in the general vicinity of the point from which the architect intended the second shot to be played) and extend through the green.

To sound like a golfer, keep this in mind: Par threes do not have an approach. And the approach on a par five can be either the second or third shot, depending upon the length of the hole and shot a player is attempting. For example, for a player attempting to reach the green in two shots, the approach would be the entire area between him and the green. If the player lays up with his second shot, the approach would be the area between the ball and the green prior to playing the third shot.

approach putt A long putt made with the intention of getting the ball close to the hole rather than actually holing out. If you really want to sound like a golfer, you would refer to such a putt as a lag putt as opposed to an *approach putt*.

approach shot Now that you know what the approach is, an *approach shot* is any shot played in an attempt to navigate the approach and reach the green. So if you hit a good drive on a par four and are playing your second shot with the intention of getting the ball on the green, you are playing your approach shot, regardless of the outcome. Got it?

apron The closely cropped grass that separates the putting green from the rough and/or fairway. The grass is cut lower than the fairway but not as low as the putting green. The term is somewhat dated, and to sound like a golfer, you would refer to this area as the fringe.

architect A person who designs golf courses—and the person you should curse out (in absentia) or applaud in the grill after your round, depending upon how you played.

architecture The practice of designing golf courses and the nature of that practice as it applies to a particular hole or course. The subject of *architecture* as it pertains to golf is popular among students of the game, and to play the game at the highest level, it is vital to understand how the design of a course impacts the way it can and should be played.

army golf When you hit one shot to the left, the next to the right, and continue with this left, right, left, right pattern, you're playing *army golf*, so called from the "left, right, left, right" cadence to which soldiers march.

Arnie's Army The legions of fans that swarmed around golf courses in pursuit of Arnold Palmer in his heyday were known as *Arnie's Army*. To say Palmer's fans were rabid would be an understatement.

attack, attacking This refers to an aggressive style of play and can indicate the overall style of a player (such as Lanny Wadkins) or the style or mind-set a player adopts for a particular shot, hole, or golf course. You'll hear this used mostly to describe something a player shouldn't do as opposed to something he should do. For example, in describing a U.S. Open venue, a player or analyst might say, "You can't *attack* this golf course. If you do, you will pay the price." What he means is that the course is not

Lanny Wadkins, here in 1977, favors an attack style of play.

one players can attempt to over-power—accuracy and course manage-ment are premium—or that the course will not present many opportunities to fire directly at the flag.

True attack players aggressively fire at the hole regardless of the layout or the circumstances. A noted teaching professional once said of Lanny Wadkins, "If the hole were cut on a Frisbee in the middle of the Pacific Ocean, Lanny would fire right at it."

attest When you vouch for a fellow competitor's score by signing his scorecard, you are *attesting* to his score.

Augusta National Golf Club Perhaps the most famous course in the United States, the Augusta National Golf Club, is the home of the Masters (see *Masters*) and is located in Augusta, Georgia. The club was founded by Bobby Jones and his pal Clifford Roberts and designed by Jones along with Dr. Alistair MacKenzie. The course is well-known to television viewers for its phenomenal condition-ing and blooming azaleas and has hosted the Masters since 1934.

automatic press A bet that players agree on prior to a round, an *automatic*

press is typically started when a team finds itself two down. A press is a bet within a bet (see *press*).

away This term refers to the ball and the player who are farthest from the hole. It is significant because the player who is *away* plays his ball first. In match play in particular, the order of play is important to strategy, and it is not uncommon—particularly on short par fours—for a savvy player to lay back off the tee to ensure that he is away for the approach shot. The

Sam Snead missed a winning putt at the 1947 U.S. Open after an infamous dispute about whether his ball was actually away.

reason for this is that some players put stock in the credo, "First on wins," which refers to the idea that the first player on the green will win the hole.

To sound like a real golfer, you should remember that away means just that—away. The player farthest from the hole always has the right to play first. So if you're on the green 60 feet from the hole and your opponent is in a bunker and only 30 feet from the hole, you're away. A common misconception is that a ball off the green is considered to be away. Of course, in a friendly round of golf, you might indicate to your companions to play up in the above situation, but in tournament play, *away means away—without exception.*

The most infamous incident involving the oft asked question of who's away took place during a play-off between Sam Snead and Lew Worsham for the 1947 U.S. Open at St. Louis Country Club. The two men were tied as they played the eighteenth hole. Worsham missed the green with his approach while Snead hit his to 25 feet. Worsham nearly holed his chip shot, and Snead rolled his putt to within roughly two feet of the hole, seemingly equidistant as that of Worsham's. As Snead stepped up to knock his putt in, Worsham said, "Are you sure you're away?" A miffed Snead called for USGA official Ike Grainger, who produced a measuring tape and determined Snead was an inch farther from the hole. After things quieted down, Snead stepped in and missed his putt. A few seconds later, Worsham holed and won the Open. Snead never won the U.S. Open, and this event was most prominent in a series of bungled near misses.

B

back There are two things that can be referred to as being *back*—the tee markers and the hole location. The tee markers are considered *back* when they are placed at the rear of the tee, as far as possible from the hole. The hole is *back* when it is cut in any position behind the middle of the green in terms of depth.

If the tee markers are back, to sound like a real golfer you would say, "It's playing back." To indicate the hole is cut in the back of the green, you would simply say, "It's back." So when you're referring to the hole position, drop the "playing."

backhander Sometimes when the ball is very close to the hole, a player will tap it in with the back of the putter. That's a *backhander*. Sometimes a player does it casually, sometimes out of anger. More—way more—than one backhander has been missed in the history of the game.

back nine The last nine holes of a golf course, assuming it's an 18-hole course. The first nine holes are the front nine. To sound like real golfer, you would refer to the *back nine* as "the back." So you might say, "I shot 35 on the back," to indicate your score for the final nine holes. However, the chances of you shooting 35 on the back are pretty slim, so that wasn't a very good example. A final note: If you're playing a nine-hole course, the author doesn't know what to tell you. It's safe to suppose you're just playing "the nine" as opposed to the front or back nine.

back side Alternative term for back nine (see *back nine*).

backspin For those who think they can't put it on their ball, *backspin* is the Holy Grail of golf—the force that makes a golf ball magically stop and, sometimes, reverse its direction once it hits the green. Although its effect is only apparent to the eye on shots when the ball hits the green and spins backward, most squarely struck shots—even by the weakest of players—have backspin on them due to the loft of the club. So why can't you see its effects all the time? Two reasons: loft and clubhead speed. When you watch the world's best players spin the ball on the green, the ball is coming into the green at an extremely steep angle (due to the loft of the club) and has been struck with extreme force. Most of the backspin has to do with the steepness of the ball's descent into the green.

Backspin is created by the loft of the club and the grooves. If the club-face is square at impact, the ball will have backspin on it no matter which club is used, including the driver. Why doesn't your driver back up in the fairway? Trajectory. Despite the fact that the ball is spinning backward, it leaps forward when it hits the ground because of the angle at which it strikes the ground. That's why even the world's best might be able to make a three-iron stop fairly quickly on a green, but they can't make it back up on its own power.

So when one of the guys in your foursome says, "I wish I could put backspin on the ball," he really means he wishes he could make the ball stop and back up on the green. Why doesn't his ball stop and back up? Probably because he doesn't generate enough clubhead speed to produce the amount of backspin necessary to make it stop. Because he doesn't generate enough clubhead speed, the ball isn't propelled high enough to stop when it hits the green.

Once in a while you'll see the pros hit a very low pitch shot that takes one or two minibounces and stops—but it doesn't roll backward. How do they do it? Backspin. Every club in your bag has loft on it, even your putter. The pros can play these shots because the club creates backspin and because they strike the ball firmly enough to create a sufficient amount of backspin to make the ball stop after a few hops. Why don't these low burners spin back once they hit the green? They aren't coming in at a steep enough angle.

backstop Under certain circumstances, a hill behind your target (the hole) can act as a *backstop*, i.e., it can serve to stop your ball and perhaps even cause it to roll back toward the hole if you hit your shot past the hole. This is particularly helpful on bunker shots. When there is a backstop beyond the hole, i.e., the green slopes toward you behind the hole, you don't have to worry about hitting the ball too softly and possibly leaving it in the bunker.

backstroke An outdated term for the backswing.

backswing The *backswing* is the part of the swing that begins when the clubhead and body start to move and turn away from the ball. When the backswing ends is not quite so clear because during the transition from the backswing to the forward swing (downswing), the clubhead is still moving back while the hips and lower body have started toward the target.

bad yardage This term refers to two things. The first is when the posted yardage is inaccurate. In other words, when the yardage on the scorecard or yardage sheet or sprinkler head is not precise, it's referred to as *bad yardage*. The second usage refers to a yardage given to a player by his caddie, which proves to be inaccurate. In many cases, the latter use is employed as an excuse by a player who doesn't wish to acknowledge that he hit a lousy shot.

baff This obsolete term referred to a shot where the club hit the ground before the ball. Today, a similar shot might be called a scuff or a dropkick. *Baff* didn't refer to an out-and-out chunk shot (see *chunk*)—it was a shot where the club glanced off the ground and still contacted the ball.

baffing spoon A term for a wooden club that was the most lofted of a set of wooden clubs called spoons. The *baffing spoon* was used primarily for approach shots. A club of this type was out-of-date before the turn of the century.

baffy The *baffy* evolved from the baffing spoon. It was a short wooden club with a lot of loft. Not much else you need to know about it.

bag If you've ever seen a painting of a famous, old Scottish caddie or a big money match from the middle of the nineteenth century, you'll notice that the caddies simply carried the clubs bundled in their arms. It's likely golf *bags* evolved out of necessity, as players started carrying more and more clubs to make up a set. Early bags were made of leather and canvas. The modern bag has a strap, intended to be slung over the shoulder, and various compartments to hold a wide range of equipment.

bag, he can play every club in the An expression that indicates a player is proficient with any club in his hand.

bag, he has every shot in the A player who *has every shot in the bag* is a superb shotmaker, able to maneuver the ball in any direction with precise control of the ball's flight. Players such as Lee Trevino, Chi Chi Rodriquez, and Amy Alcott are said to have every shot in the bag.

bag, in his When a player is capable of playing a particular shot—for instance, he can hit a fade when the situation dictates—you might say of him, "He's got that shot *in his bag.*"

bag, in the Since there is a fourteen-club limit for tournament golf, it is not at all uncommon for top-level players to decide which fourteen clubs they will use in a tournament based on the venue for the week. For instance, a player may elect to remove the two-iron from his total of fourteen and add a five-wood if he feels the five-wood may improve his chances on certain holes. The most famous example of this was Raymond Floyd's runaway victory in the 1976 Masters, when he had a five-wood *in the bag,* which he used to savage the par fives at Augusta National.

bag, on the A caddie working for a player is said to be *on the bag* for that player. For example, a television analyst might say, "Bruce Edwards is on the bag for Tom Watson."

bag, solid through the This is a very good thing to be. If you're *solid through the bag,* it means you can hit every club and every shot you might possibly face.

bag boy At some private clubs, the *bag boy* is an employee who retrieves clubs from the bag storage room prior to the members' rounds. At most private clubs, a member will pull his auto into the vicinity of the clubhouse, and the bag boy will take the clubs from the trunk of the vehicle or place them in the trunk—depending on whether the member is coming or going and, if he's going, if he's taking his clubs with him. If the member is leaving his bag at the club, the bag boy will put the clubs in bag storage after the clubs are cleaned. If the member has a caddie, the caddie will do the cleaning and storing.

bag cover There are two types of *bag covers*. The first typically snaps to the top of the bag and is used to cover the clubs when it starts to rain. The second is a cover that envelopes the entire bag and is commonly used to protect a golf bag during airline travel.

bag drop At some golf clubs, there is an area where a player will pull up in his car and be met by the bag boy (see *bag boy*), who will take the clubs from the player and get them into a marshalling area where the player can find his bag ready to go to the first tee, typically after changing his shoes.

bag rack Any rack, typically made of wood or metal piping, designed to lean a bag against in an upright position.

bag rat Slang for caddie.

bag room A room, sometimes outfitted with stacked, horizontal shelving, where bags are stored for the membership at a private club or for visitors who will be playing a few consecutive days at a resort.

bag stand A *bag stand* is a device against which a golf bag leans in order to stand upright. Some modern carry bags (see *carry bag*) have collapsible bag stands attached to the front of them, which keeps the bag upright when the player removes the bag from his shoulder. It retracts when the player picks the bag up again.

bag tag A tag, typically made of plastic (sometimes of wood or leather), which bears the seal of a particular golf club and is hung on a player's bag to denote the fact that the player is a member at the club or is playing at the club as a guest or visitor. In some cases, the *bag tag* is coded with the player's bag storage number, which corresponds to a slot or rack in the bag room.

bailout A bailout is not a particularly good shot, nor is it an excessively poor shot. A *bailout* occurs when, at the last microsecond, a player decides to play away from serious trouble on a hole, such as water, out-of-bounds, or a truly severe bunker, and in doing so plays the ball in the extreme opposite direction. Top-level players are aware of their propensity for doing this and often select a safe area, away from the trouble, where a shot of this nature will hopefully land. Since a bailout is in reality a less than perfect shot, the player cannot always accurately predict where it will go.

bailout area The area where a player is hopeful his ball will land in the event that he chickens out at the last minute and hits a bailout. Some architects design *bailout areas* into a certain hole so that the safe option is available for average players and for top-level players who lose their nerve at the last second.

balata ball The *balata* part of this term refers to a substance originally derived from the gum of the bully or balata tree of northeastern South America and the West Indies. The soft balata cover on a ball made it perfect for top-level players because it offered tremendous spin and feel. The drawback of genuine balata was that the soft cover cut easily during mis-hit iron shots when the lead edge of the club contacted the ball. Today, synthetic balata is used to make *balata balls*. The synthetic material retains the original advantages of the substance but is more resistant to cutting.

ball It's the white thing you try to hit and try to get into the hole in the fewest possible shots. If you need more information about it than that, try bowling.

ball, be the Chevy Chase's character in *Caddyshack* encouraged caddie Danny Noonan to *be the ball*. It doesn't mean anything, but golfers love to say it.

ball, good An expression used to let another player know you think he hit a good shot.

ball, nice Similar to the above, it can also be used to talk about a player's overall game, as in, "He hits a *nice ball.*"

ball at rest When your ball is sitting motionless on the ground, it's *at rest*. If you cause it to move while it's at rest (unless you're striking at it with the intent to play a shot), it's a penalty.

Ballesteros, Severiano One of the most exciting players to watch in the entire history of the game, Ballesteros emerged from Spain in the mid-1970s and brought excitement back to the professional game at a level not known since Arnold Palmer was at his peak. His game and emotions were similar to Palmer's as well—they ran the gamut from miserable to extraordinary and were visible for all to see. Ballesteros

AP/WIDE WORLD PHOTOS

Severiano Ballesteros at the 1996 British Open.

may well be the most naturally talented player in the game's history and was renowned for his shotmaking and imagination. He won five major championships—three British Opens and two Masters.

ball flight The action of your ball in the air is its *ball flight*. Many things influence the ball's flight, but the most significant factor is the angle of the clubface at impact.

ballmaker Back in the early days of golf, a *ballmaker* was a craftsman along the lines of a clubmaker. Obviously, he made golf balls—one at a time.

ball mark When a ball lands on a green, it often makes a small impres-sion in the green. Such an impres-sion is called a *ball mark*. You can and should fix it with a tee or a small metal tool designed for this purpose.

ball marker On the green, it is per-missible to place a marker behind your ball so you can lift it and clean it and/or get it out of the way of some-one else's line of putt (see *line of putt*). All real golfers use a small coin as a *ball marker*. Just remember: You place the marker behind the ball, and when you replace the ball, it goes in front of the marker.

balloon A shot that flies higher than typical for the club with which it was struck is said to *balloon*. It's a silly term, even for golf. You'll sound more like a real golfer if you just say, "It flew higher than I expected," or if you use the term *upshoot* (see *upshoot*). Also, you might hear someone say, "I tried to *balloon one* over a tree." Forget it—just say, "I tried to hit it over the tree."

ball position When you take your address position (see *address*), the ball's relationship to your feet is known as the *ball position*. If the ball is closer to your front foot than your back foot, it's forward. If it's closer to your back foot, it's back. If the ball is equidistant from your two feet, it's middle. Your ball position varies depending on what type of shot you're playing.

ball retriever A telescopic device outfitted with a small tool on the end so that golf balls can be fished out of the water. Real golfers don't own *ball retrievers*, but if you know someone who has one, here's a good line to use on them: "Hey, Fred, I hear your wife had your ball retriever regripped for your birthday." Knocks 'em dead every time.

ballstriking The act of hitting full shots (see *full*), no matter which club you use, is known as *ballstriking*. A player who excels at this part of the game—separate from putting, chipping, and pitching (see *putt, chip, pitch*)—is known as a great *ballstriker*.

ball washer A device, typically located near the tee box, into which a ball is placed and scrubbed clean in soapy water by tiny brushes located inside the unit. Some *ball washers* operate by pumping a handle, located on the top, up and down, while others work by turning a crank on the side. Ordinarily, a towel of some sort is attached to the side of the unit so the player can dry the ball.

banana ball A completely out-of-control, left-to-right shot that ends up well right of the intended target. This is no ordinary slice—it's a major-league slice.

bang A long tee shot is sometimes said to have been *banged*.

bap-headed The shape of a wood from the late nineteenth and early twentieth century, distinct because of its round, flat shape, as opposed to the long-nosed woods of earlier eras. This term is also an excellent impairment to accuse your partner of having after he misses a two-footer to halve a hole (see *halve*), i.e., "What are you, *bap-headed* or something?"

bare lie If you have a *bare lie*, it means there is no grass under the ball. Be careful you don't skull it (see *skull*).

barky Anytime your ball comes in contact with a tree and you still make a par on the hole, you've made a *barky*. (Trees have bark on them. Get it?)

barranca This term is a Spanish word for a rocky ravine or gully. Sometimes the *barranca* has water in it; sometimes it doesn't. If you were playing in California, you might hit your ball into a barranca. In New York, you'd hit it into a ditch. Either way, it's not a good place to be.

Barry Burn A small creek (*burn* is the Scottish equivalent of creek or stream), Barry Burn fronts the eighteenth green at Carnoustie Golf Club in Scotland. The final hole at Carnoustie is a 460-yard par four, considered one of the toughest championship par fours on one of the world's most difficult championship courses.

baseball grip A method of holding the golf club similar to the way a baseball bat is gripped (unless you hold a bat like Ty Cobb). The hands touch, but no fingers interlock or overlap. The *baseball grip* is sometimes referred to as the ten-finger grip.

beach, on the Slang for the sand in most bunkers. A player who seemed to be in the sand frequently during his round might lament that he spent too much time *on the beach*.

Beardies, the A series of four bunkers in the fourteenth fairway of the Old Course (see *Old Course*), the Beardies dictate the tee shot on one of the world's most famous par four holes.

beater Slang for an old, worn ball, particularly one you might pluck out of the water or find buried in the ground. If you were playing golf in Massachusetts, it would be a "beetah."

Also, a bad player is sometimes referred to as a *beater*.

beating balls When you hit practice balls, you are *beating balls*.

beer cart One of the great innovations of the modern era, the *beer cart* is a motorized vehicle that travels around some courses selling food and other vital nutritional elements such as beer.

bellied wedge Sometimes a ball comes to rest against the edge of the rough surrounding the green. The ideal shot would be played along the ground with a putter. However, it's difficult to get the head of the putter smoothly through the rough. The solution is a *bellied wedge*, which is a shot played with a sand wedge using a putting stroke. The ball is contacted on its belly (center) with the lead edge of the club (see *lead edge*).

bend If you *bend* the ball, you make it curve either from right to left or left to right. If the hole you're playing *bends*, it curves in one direction or the other. If you slam your club on the ground and the shaft *bends*, you have to take it out of play. If you *bend* your club in the normal course of play, i.e., if you hit a tree root while playing a shot and the shaft gets a kink in it, you can continue to use it or fix it without undue delay. Exactly how you fix a bent shaft without undue delay is beyond the author's comprehension.

bent Short for bent grass. See below.

bent grass A type of thin-bladed grass used on many championship golf courses, particularly in the northern and northeastern parts of the United States. *Bent grass* is very resilient (except in extreme heat) and can be mowed very short, which makes it superb for fairways and greens.

bent greens Greens of bent grass. It can be safely said that, in the United States, *bent greens* are *the* preferred surface for championship play.

Berg, Patty One of the founding members of the LPGA (see *Ladies Professional Golf Association*), Berg won 57 tournaments in her career, including 15 women's major championships. Berg was one of the four original inductees into the LPGA Hall of Fame in 1951.

Bermuda grass This type of grass grows well in warm climates and is used throughout much of the southern United States where it is very difficult to maintain bent grass. *Bermuda* is a thick-bladed grass that, when grown high for rough, is particularly punish-

Patty Berg, here in 1943, was one of the biggest female golf stars of the 1930s and '40s.

ing because the ball typically sinks down to the roots of the grass rather than perching on top.

be right When your ball appears headed toward the hole, you can ask it to *be right* just in case it gets any ideas about not stopping near the hole.

best ball When partners are playing in a best-ball match, the lowest score

20

of the two on a given hole is their *best ball*. Typically, the score of this ball is matched against the best ball of the opponents, and the two high scores are irrelevant. In some betting matches, three players will pit their best ball (the lowest of the three) against the score of a single player. A *best-ball match* is any match contested and scored in this manner, sometimes referred to as a four-ball match, particularly outside of the United States.

bet A *bet* in golf is the same as in any other endeavor—a challenge which rewards the winner with a prize, typically money. Lee Trevino once said, "Pressure is playing a match for ten

Lee Trevino famously enjoyed the pressure of a bet.

PGA TOUR

dollars when you only have five in your pocket."

better ball Just another way of referring to best ball (see *best ball*).

between clubs Sometimes a shot is of a distance that is *between clubs*—that is, the distance to be covered is longer than you can hit it with one club but shorter than you would hit it with the next club in your set.

beveled edge A *beveled edge* is a lead edge (see *lead edge*), typically on a wedge, which is ground off rather than at a sharp angle.

big banger If you hit the ball a long way from the tee, you're a *big banger*.

big hitter A player who hits the ball greater distances than considered typical is a *big hitter*.

big number When you make a high score for a hole or a round, you might just say you made a *big number* to avoid telling anyone how bad things really were.

Billy Baroo Ted Knight's character in *Caddyshack* had a putter he called *Billy Baroo*. Prior to the big putt on the last hole of the match, Knight caressed the putter and whispered to it, "Oh, Billy, Billy, Billy, Billy, Billy . . ."

bingle bangle bongle A betting game with three points available on each hole. The first point is awarded to the person who hits the green in the fewest strokes, the second point to the closest to the hole once all are on the green, and the third to the first person to hole out. Ties are worth half a point. In some necks of the woods, *bingle bangle bongle* is referred to as *bingo bango bongo*.

bird Short for birdie, which is a score of one under par on a given hole.

bird dog A *bird dog* is any caddie who acts as a forecaddie, staying out ahead of the players so he can see precisely where all the balls in the group come to rest.

birdie A score of one under par on a hole. The term dates back to its everyday use at the turn of the century when just about anything good was referred to as a bird. In the history book *Fifty Years of American Golf* (published in 1936), author H. B. Martin cites a tale from 1899, as told by Ab Smith (whoever he was): ". . . my ball . . . came to rest within six inches of the cup. I said 'that was a bird of a

shot. . . . I suggest that when one of us plays a hole in one under par he receives double compensation.' The other two agreed and we began right away, just as soon as the next one came, to call it a birdie."

birdieable Term used to describe a hole that the expert player believes he can easily birdie (see *birdie*). Also referred to as a *birdie hole*.

bird's nest This is a lie in the rough where the ball sits down and is surrounded by grass on all sides so that it resembles an egg in a bird's nest. If you regularly play in a tough group, the author recommends against frequent use of this term—unless you hit your ball in an actual bird's nest.

bisque Aside from being an excellent variety of soup, a *bisque* is something you should leap at the chance to take when offered by an opponent in a betting match. It is a floating handicap stroke that you can take at any point in the match. Obviously, this is a specialized betting handicap and wouldn't be used in any type of tournament play.

bite More often than not, this term is muttered or yelled by a player who wants his ball to stop immediately upon hitting the green. A shot that stops in such a manner is also said to have *bite*. Here's a bonus tip: If you have to ask a putt to bite, you're in trouble—but your playing companions will get a good laugh out of it.

blade Like many golf terms, this one has multiple uses. When all irons were forged steel, the head of the club was referred to as the *blade*. As the design of clubs evolved, so too did the use of this term, so that today *blade*, at least as it refers to irons, is used only to describe forged irons. Also, the putter has long been referred to as *the blade* in slang.

In contrast to its meaning as a noun, which brings to mind images of the classic and stylish lines of forged irons, its meaning as a verb is ugly. If you *blade* a shot, it means you've contacted the ball with the lead edge of an iron—that is, you've thinned it, skulled it, hit it skinny—sending it on a low trajectory with too much force. Any way you look at it, it stinks.

blade putter Different from the general slang use above, if you hear someone refer to a blade as opposed to the blade, they are describing a certain type of putter, one which has the same basic construction in the head and

Ben Crenshaw, here in 1984, uses a blade putter.

neck as a forged iron. It is not uncommon for the term to be used in tandem with the word *classic*, as in *classic blade putter*. Blade putters were fairly standard prior to the advent of perimeter-weighted putters.

blast A common misconception is that every shot played from the sand is a blast shot, but that's not the case. A *blast* is played only when the ball is buried or is too close to the lip to play a standard bunker shot. Typically, the ball is positioned in the center of the stance or just right of center, and there is little or no follow-through. In this sense, the term refers to the impact's resemblance to a miniature explosion, with more sand being contacted than during the skimming action of a typical bunker shot.

You can also hit a blast outside of the sand. *Blast* is also a slang term for a long drive, i.e., a big *blast*.

blind shot Although from time to time we all play as if we can't see, in golf, *blind* refers to a hole or a particular shot in which the target is not clearly visible. Modern designs tend to shy away from *blind shots*, but the hidden target was a basic design element through the 1930s.

block When you *block* a shot, it flies to the right of your target, either a straight push or a slice. However, the term does not refer to the flight of the ball, but rather to the player's failure to release the right side (or the blocking of the right side) of the body through the ball. This often results in an open clubface at impact, which results in the ball flights mentioned above.

blood, no In match play situations when neither side wins a given hole, there's *no blood*, i.e., no one has suffered as a result of the tie.

blow a lead Just like everything else in life, if you screw up in golf, you blow it. So if you're winning your match or winning a tournament and you inexplicably collapse, what you did was *blow the lead*. But don't feel bad—Greg Norman made a career out of doing the same.

blow up This is what you're doing while you're in the midst of blowing a lead. More often than not, you *blow up* under pressure, so this is a nice way of saying you choked.

blue tees Traditionally, the tee block markers for the championship or professional tees were painted blue, thus they were called the *blue tees* or simply the *blues*.

Bob Barker For many years, Bob Barker was the host of a television game show (*The Price Is Right*) in which contestants from the studio audience were invited to "come on down" in order to play. If you hit a shot too high and you want it to "come on down," you've hit yourself a *Bob Barker*.

Bo Derek Ms. Derek was the star of a motion picture called *10,* which not only described her physical attributes but is also the number traditionally assigned to perfection in athletics scored by judges. So if you think you've hit a perfect shot, you've hit a *Bo Derek*.

body English If your putt is breaking to the left and you find yourself leaning to the left in an effort to "help" the ball in, your using *body English*. Just be careful you don't fall over.

bogey A score of one over par for a given hole. So if you're playing a par four and you take five strokes, you've made a *bogey*. Where's the word come from? It is believed to be derived from a British music hall tune which was popular prior to the turn of the century. The song included a line warning, "Here comes the Bogey Man, he'll catch you if he can." The ever proper Brits assigned the Bogey Man the rank of colonel and for a time referred to him as Colonel Bogey, who was an imaginary competitor who played the course at an attainable standard of good play for an average golfer. So if bogey was the standard, why do we now use par as a measurement for standard good play? Actually, par is a standard for excellent play, which is how it came into use. Early in the century, American clubs assigned a par and bogey score for each hole, so

expert and average players would have a mark to measure themselves against. As a result, when the expert player failed to match par on a hole but did make the bogey score, he looked at the hole as a failure, hence the word bogey evolved from something that was okay into something players really looked at in a negative sense.

Having said all that, once you've made that bogey, you've *bogeyed* the hole. More than one bogey and you are making *bogeys*.

bogey competition Back when bogey was considered a good score in the British Isles, clubs held *bogey competitions* wherein the players' scores were matched against bogey in match play competition. For example, if bogey for a hole was considered five and the player made a five, the hole was halved. If the player made six he lost the hole to his imaginary foe, and if he made four, he won the hole. Who won the contest? Whoever beat old Colonel Bogey by the largest margin. This style of competition gradually fell from popularity in favor of stroke play.

bogey train Ever have one of those days when it seems as if you can't buy a par? Well, when you're making bogey after bogey after bogey, you're on the *bogey train*. Sometimes in an

effort to explain poor play, an excellent player might say, "I got on board the bogey train and just couldn't get off."

bolt Make a putt that's moving real fast at the hole, or make a short one with a firm, confident stroke, and you've *bolted* it.

bomb When you hit a shot a long way, you've *bombed* it. The term is borrowed from other sports where just about anything that goes a long way (a home run in baseball, a long pass in American football) is a *bomb*.

boron A synthetic element typically added to the tips of graphite shafts to prevent the shafts from breaking or shattering.

borrow When you borrow something, the idea is that you intend to give it back. In golf, the amount you *borrow* refers to the amount of break you play on a putt. So if you think a putt is going to curve six inches on its journey to the hole, you borrow six inches in the hope that the ball will return it and fall in the hole. If you overestimated the amount of break (the putt actually only broke four inches), you are said to have borrowed too much. If you underestimated the break of the putt (it actually broke eight inches), you haven't borrowed enough.

boss of the moss Any player who is a good putter is the *boss of the moss*, since a closely mown green somewhat resembles moss. American professional Loren Roberts carries this nickname on tour due to his putting proficiency.

SAM GREENWOOD/PGA TOUR

Loren Roberts's talent on the greens has earned him the nickname "Boss of the Moss."

bounce The *bounce* is the curvature on the bottom or sole of a sand wedge (see *sand wedge*), which helps prevent too much of the club from coming in contact with the sand and allows the clubhead to move easily through the sand, in combination with the flange (see *flange*).

bowed If at the top of your swing your left wrist is drooped toward the ground, it is *bowed*, and it's not a good thing.

box grooves Grooves on the face of a club that are made, depthwise, in the shape of a U are sometimes referred to as *box grooves*. Grooves of this shape (particularly those on the Karsten Manufacturing Company's Ping Eye 2 irons, which featured a rounded edge on its box grooves) created a major controversy in the late 1980s because of their alleged ability to create more spin on shots played from the rough. Despite this, box grooves are legal.

bramble Today, golf balls have dimples. Late in the gutta-percha period of golf balls and early in the rubber core era, balls didn't have dimples. Instead, they had *bramble*, raised dots that helped to lift the ball into the air. The term comes from the name of the prickly bushes on which blackberries grow. Blackberries, of course, appear to be a cluster of raised bumps.

brassie A wooden club, fitted with a brass sole plate (hence the name), that has more loft than a spoon (three-

wood) and less loft than a driver. When wooden clubs began being stamped with numbers, a brassie was a two-wood.

break This term has two basic uses within the game. The first refers to the amount that a putt will curve as it makes its way toward the hole. In this sense, *break* can also refer to the general lay of a green or a portion of the green. If a putt will move three inches from left to right as it moves toward the hole, it is said to have three inches of *break*. While it's actually in motion, it is *breaking*. After you've made the putt (we're thinking positive here), you will brag to your friends that it *broke* three inches.

The second usage of the term refers to a movement the wrists make during the backswing. Just after the moment the club starts to move upward—that is, at the moment the club stops its progression in a straight line away from the ball—the wrists must *break*, or cock upward, in order to allow the backswing to continue. The wrists remain in this position until late in the downswing.

breakfast ball A variation on the term *mulligan* (see *mulligan*), a *breakfast ball* is a second tee shot on the first hole, which allows the player to discount the original ball. This practice came into being because players are often stiff or have a belly full of scrambled eggs and sausage, which prevents a flexible swing.

British Amateur The amateur championship of Great Britain, it was one of golf's four original major championships (see *major championship*).

British ball A ball of not more than 1.62 inches in diameter and with a weight of not more than 1.62 ounces, it was the standard ball in all R & A competitions prior to the early 1970s, after which the American ball was adapted for use in R & A competitions.

British Open The oldest of golf's four major championships, the British Open was first contested in 1860, which makes it by far the oldest and most historic golf championship in the world. It is conducted by the Royal and Ancient Golf Club (see *Royal and Ancient Golf Club*) and boasts the strongest international field of all championships. In the modern era, it has been conducted over the same basic rotation of courses (see *rota*).

brogue An iron spike with a wooden handle (the two joined to form a "T") used to stuff boiled feathers inside the

John Daly celebrates a birdie putt at the 1995 British Open on the Old Course at St. Andrews. He later won the tournament after a four-hole playoff.

leather casings in the construction of featherie balls.

broom Players sometimes refer to putting as *brooming*, i.e., "I *broomed* in a ten-footer for birdie at the third hole."

brother-in-law act A variation of ham-and-egg (see *ham-and-egg*), the term describes the tendency of partners to seemingly coordinate alternating spurts of good play so that one player plays

28

well while the other plays bad, and then the latter player comes on when the former starts to wobble a bit.

bucket Almost any bunch of practice balls is referred to as a *bucket* of balls, dating to the days when driving ranges (see *driving range*) doled out balls in wire baskets or buckets.

build a stance You are entitled, under the Rules of Golf, to firmly plant your feet prior to playing a shot, but you cannot *build a stance*. This means you can't put stuff under your feet (or knees, as Craig Stadler learned in the 1987 San Diego Open when he put a towel under his knees before playing a shot from under a tree). It also means, especially in hazards, that you can't move stuff like rocks and twigs from underfoot once you've taken your stance.

bulge If you still have a persimmon driver, take a close look at the face of it. You'll notice that the face isn't flat. In fact, it is convex from both top to bottom and side to side. Neat, huh? That curve from side to side (toe to heel) is called *bulge*, and it's the reason you hit a hook when you hit the ball out on the toe.

bulge and roll Still looking at that driver? Good. Now that you know

what bulge is, roll is the curve from top to bottom. Together, these two curves on the face of the wooden club are called *bulge and roll*.

bump and run A shot played to run almost entirely along the ground, the idea being that the player *bumps* the ball with the clubhead and the ball then *runs* along the ground to the green.

bunker If you want to sound like a real golfer, there's no such thing as a sand trap. But it's a little more complicated than that, you see, because some bunkers have no sand in them, and not all sandy areas are bunkers. So here's some rules for you to figure out: If it has sand in it, even if it's shallow, and you can easily identify where it

Doug Sanders hits out of a bunker

begins and ends, it's a *bunker* and a hazard. If it looks like a pit, it's a *bunker*, whether it has sand or not. If the bunker is *sans* sand, it is not a hazard, so you can ground your club and all the other good stuff you normally do when your ball is sitting on grass. The rules only acknowledge bunkers with sand as hazards.

Some modern courses incorporate something known as a waste area or waste bunker in their design. These areas typically run next to a fairway and are rather substantial in size—big enough to comfortably accommodate several hundred people for a day at the beach. Waste areas are typically defined as such on the scorecard from the course, and the distinction is important. In a bunker filled with sand (a hazard), you cannot ground your club or move any loose impediments. In a waste area, you can do both.

If your ball lands in a bunker, you have *bunkered* it. The bunkers on a hole or an entire golf course are referred to as its *bunkering*.

bunt An exceptionally short shot, when a longer one was called for, is a *bunt*. The term is borrowed from baseball.

buried lie Any time your ball is almost entirely covered by sand or grass, that's a *buried lie*. Be sure to eat your Wheaties before tackling it.

burner Any tee shot that's hit hard—particularly a low-flying one—is a *burner*.

burn the edge When a putt hits any part of the circumference of the hole without falling in, it has *burned the edge*. If you just couldn't get a putt to drop all day, but had a lot that were close, you might confide to your beer mug, "I burned the edges all day." Your beer will understand. Doesn't it always?

Bushwood Country Club The fictional country club (see *country club*) that served as the setting for the film *Caddyshack* (see *Caddyshack*).

butt The end of the shaft over which the hands are placed is sometimes called the *butt* end of the club. Also, the top of that end of the club is referred to as the *butt*.

butterfly with sore feet, like a A delicate shot that lands ever so softly on the green and doesn't roll much is said to have landed *like a butterfly with sore feet*.

bye The low qualifiers in a match-play event are sometimes given a *bye* in the first round of a tournament, i.e., they do not have to play a match in the first round and move automatically to the second round.

bye holes In match play, the holes still to be played on the course when a match is decided before the eighteenth hole. More often than not, players simply cease playing when the match is over. So if you win your match on the fifteenth hole (nice job), the sixteenth, seventeenth, and eighteenth are *bye holes*.

C

cabbage Slang for exceedingly long grass or a particularly nasty lie in the rough.

caddie A person who carries a golfer's bag during a round, often providing course information (yardages), suggestions (which club to hit, which way a putt breaks), and service (raking bunkers, replacing divots). Also, the act of working as a caddie. The term is derived from the French *cadet*, a page to military officers. If you want to sound like and act like a real golfer, make sure you ask your caddie his name before the round begins and use

it. Don't refer to him as Caddie as if it was the name he was given at birth.

caddie bag A small, light golf bag that a club player uses when employing a caddie. More popular when large, tour-style bags were popular among the country club set.

caddie cart Outdated term for a golf cart.

caddie dip This slang term from swing mechanics has no precise definition but refers an excessive "dip" or lowering of the knees toward the ball at impact. The implication is that a player with this type of move through impact learned to play as a caddie and had no former schooling in the proper technique of the golf swing. You won't see many *caddie dips* on tour, but one famous player that did have a noticeable dip was Tony Lema, the 1964 British Open champion. The caddie dip was much more prevalent when world-class players sought to achieve the reverse C position at impact, a goal that is no longer considered prudent among golfologists.

caddie master or **caddymaster** An employee of a golf club who assigns caddies to players and performs other services for the membership. There was a time when the caddie master received a percentage of the fee the caddie was paid, typically 10 percent. This practice has, for the most part, been abandoned.

caddie scholarship In certain geographic regions, golfers donate money to a scholarship fund for caddies. The caddie must be recommended by his club, and such a recommendation is typically based upon number of years of loyal service to the club and its membership. The two most famous *caddie scholarship* funds are the Evans Fund in Chicago, named for the great

amateur Charles "Chick" Evans and the J. Wood Platt Fund in Philadelphia, also named for a famous amateur golfer.

caddyshack A building on the grounds of a golf club where caddies wait to be assigned their bags. Any caddie worth his salt would simply refer to the building as the shack. Some *caddyshacks* have card tables, which allow the caddies to partake in their favorite pastime, namely, trying to win money from other caddies.

Caddyshack One of the few motion pictures about golf considered a classic, this film from Warner Brothers depicted the shenanigans at the fictional Bushwood Country Club. The movie starred Bill Murray, Chevy Chase, Ted Knight, and Rodney Dangerfield.

Calamity Jane Nickname for the hickory-shafted blade putter used by Bobby Jones as well as replicas of that putter. Also, if your partner is named Jane, it's something you might say after she snap hooks her drive out-of-bounds, as in, "That's a real calamity, Jane."

Calcutta Golfers love to bet, typically on themselves. But in a *Calcutta*, the members of a club buy teams at an auction for an event. The total funds from the auction are then pooled and distributed in percentages to the owners of the winning team and, typically, the teams finishing second and third in the event. As you might imagine, a Calcutta can involve quite a bit of money.

callaway or **calloway** A method of scoring for golf outings and informal events, which handicaps players based on their score for the day, regardless of whether they hold an official handicap. The system eliminates scores for entire holes based on the player's total score. The key to winning a *callaway* is to shoot a decent score for the round but make a few bad scores on certain holes. But don't make your bad ones too bad. Any score more than twice the par of a hole can't be thrown out.

can Slang for the hole or for the act of holing a putt that's made with a supremely confident stroke. When you make a putt of this nature, you've *canned* it. When talking to your ball in an effort to will it into the hole, you might say, "Get in the *can.*"

card Short for scorecard, which is the piece of paper on which you record your score and/or your fellow com-

petitor's score, depending upon the event. Also, the piece of paper you tear up in disgust after a poor round or the one you fling onto the table in the grillroom so bets can be tallied and settled. Most scorecards have boxes to record scores for each hole and totals for the front nine, back nine, and the full eighteen. Scorecards also indicate the handicap rating of the holes and the yardages of the holes from each set of tees, as well as the total yardage for the nines and the eighteen from each set of tees.

To sound like a real player, you would refer to your score after the round by saying, "I *carded* a 76." (Nice round, bud.) Sometimes, however, things don't go the way we'd like in golf, and we are a bit nonplussed with the outcome of a given round. The solution to this is a *no card*, which means you've chosen not to post your score for consideration in the event. A no card is indicated in the final tally with two simple but horrifying letters, NC.

careered it When you hit a shot as good as you possibly can, you might say you *careered it,* meaning you've never hit one better.

career round The round a player considers his best ever is his *career round.* This doesn't necessarily mean it's the lowest score he's ever shot—just the best round he's ever played taking into account things such as pressure and the event. For example, your career round might be the one time you beat your arch rival, even if you shot a high score in doing so.

Carner, JoAnne A five-time winner of the U.S. Women's Amateur and winner of forty-two professional events, Carner was one of the most popular figures in the history of the LPGA (see *LPGA*). She was player of the year three times and won the Vare Trophy (see *Vare Trophy*) for low scoring aver-

JoAnne Carner reacts to a missed putt at a 1997 LPGA tournament.

AP/WIDE WORLD PHOTOS

age five times. Carner also won two U.S. Women's Opens and is the only player to have won the U.S. Girls' Junior, U.S. Women's Amateur, and U.S. Women's Open in a career. Her nickname before she married was the Great Gundy, which she was tagged with during her dominant amateur career. (Her maiden name was Gunderson.) As of this writing, she is still the last amateur to win an LPGA Tour event, the 1969 Burdine's Invitational in Miami.

carpet Slang for both the fairway and the green. A player who hits a fairway or green in regulation might say, "I'm on the *carpet*."

carry The distance a ball flies in the air or the act of a ball safely clearing a hazard or obstacle. The word *carry*, as it relates to objects flying through the air, dates to medieval times when it referred to the distance arrows would have to fly to clear the wall of a castle. To use this term properly, you would say things such as, "That drive *carried* 230 yards," which would indicate how far it flew in the air before touching the ground. Or you might inquire of your caddie, "How far to *carry* that bunker?" His answer would be the yardage that the shot you are about to attempt would have to fly in the air to safely clear that bunker.

carryover In betting games, the value of a hole that is tied is added (carried over) to the value of the subsequent hole or holes. The *carryover* is an important element of betting matches because it makes every hole significant.

cart Short for golf cart, a motorized vehicle designed to carry two players and two golf bags.

cart barn Carts, being the strange animals that they are, need a place to rest when they aren't out grazing on the course. The storage area for carts is called the *cart barn*, which is where electric carts are hooked up to batteries overnight to charge them in preparation for following day. If you've ever accidentally staggered into a cart barn and heard a strange buzzing in your ears, it's the batteries charging—not the martini you had after the round.

cart girl The beer cart (see *beer cart*) at most clubs is typically operated by an attractive woman—the *cart girl*—with whom every male golfer typically falls in love. After all, she does have the beer.

cart golf When two golfers occupying the same cart hit their tee shots in the same vicinity, that's *cart golf*, so called because the players don't have to drive back and forth between balls. Cart golf is purely accidental.

cart path A paved, loose gravel or dirt path designed for motorized golf carts to drive on from tee to green. The *cart path* interjects itself into the game in a variety of ways, not the least of which is creating problems for the golfer as he takes his stance. A paved cart path is an immovable obstruction, and you can take relief if your ball is on one or you have to stand on one while addressing the ball. If the path has rails or sides or whatever, they are considered part of the path. If the path is just a well-worn dirt path, it's up to local rules to determine if you get relief.

If your ball hits a cart path and bounces an extra 50 yards, good for you. If it hits a cart path and bounces OB (see *OB*), that's just tough luck, pal.

casting from the top This is something you definitely don't want to do. If someone tells you, "You're *casting from the top*," they mean that you are beginning your downswing with a lazy arm swing, including a premature uncocking of the wrists, which can only lead to a weak slap at the ball and a puny slice. You've got to get your lower body into the act when you're casting from the top.

casual water This a fancy way of saying puddle. *Casual water* is any water on a course that isn't part of a hazard, and you're entitled to relief from it. So if it rains a whole bunch and the ground is soggy in some parts and puddled in others, how do you know what is considered casual water and what is simply considered soggy ground? Well, if you can see water before or after you take your stance, it's casual water, and you can take relief. That means that if there isn't any water on the surface but your body weight causes water to come to the surface, you're in casual water. And perhaps you ought to lay off the nachos, too.

cavity back When perimeter-weighted irons (see *perimeter-weighted irons*) were first introduced, there was a noticeable cavity on the back of the club since the weight and the mass of the club were concentrated around the outside edges of the club. Such clubs came to be commonly called *cavity back* clubs.

CC An abbreviation for country club (see *country club*).

cellophane bridge Ever hit a putt with proper pace that looked as if it went right over the hole and didn't drop? What prevented it from falling in the hole? Well, the *cellophane bridge*, of course. You can't see it, but your ball took it. The toll is an extra stroke on the hole.

Center City When you crack one right down the middle of the fairway, that's *Center City*, baby.

center cut A putt that rolls directly into the middle of the hole with certainty is referred to as *center cut,* an allusion to the finest cuts of meat, which are also called center cuts.

center-shafted If the head of a putter is joined with the shaft in the middle of the clubhead, it is a *center-shafted* putter. It's against the Rules of Golf for any club other than a putter to be so shafted.

Central America putt Your ball is creeping toward the hole, destined, it seems, to go in. But it doesn't. It stops one turn, or one revolution, short of its goal. With just one more revolution, you're ball would have fallen into the hole. It's a joke, you see? Central America? Revolutions?

championship tees Typically, the *championship tees* are the tees from which a hole plays its longest and that are, theoretically, the most challenging for competition. Also referred to as the blues (see *blue tees*).

Chapman system A format of play in which two partners drive from the tee and then switch balls for the second shot—A plays B's ball and B plays A's ball. After the second shots are struck, the two decide which ball is in better position and then play that ball at alternate shots until holing out.

charge When you *charge* a putt, it means you hit it with more than enough force to get it to the hole. While this is not an altogether bad thing, more often than not it is used to describe an aggressive putt that misses. If you charge a putt that goes in, you might say you *rammed* it or *canned* it.

Now when Johnny Oneputt has you four down with five to play, and you win those five holes and win the match, you *charged* back to win the match. While you were doing it, you were *charging*. For it to be a genuine charge, however, there has to be an element of drama involved, or at the very least you have to be Arnold Palmer. So if you're one down after two holes and you eventually win an evenly contested match one up, you didn't really charge back.

chariot Slang for golf cart.

chase after it A player is said to *chase after it* when his arms are fully extended early in the follow-through, the idea being that the clubhead *chases after* the ball.

chaser A *chaser* is any shot from a long way off the green that is played with the hopes that it will hit the ground running and roll up onto the green.

check up A ball *checks up* when it hits the green and stops, most often against the wishes of the player who struck it. But when a ball *checks up*, it isn't always a bad thing. Here's the difference: When you hit a full shot from the fairway, you might not want it to *check up*; you might want it to bite (see *bite*). In other words, when you use *check up* as it relates to a full shot, it means it came up short. However, on a chip or pitch that you've hit a bit too hard, you might ask your ball to *check,* meaning you want it to take a few short bounces and stop.

chew If you've grown tired of asking those overcooked nine-irons to bite, you might consider pleading with them to *chew*. The two slang terms mean the same thing, and both work best when used at high decibel levels.

chili-dip When you have a short little chip and you stick the club in the ground behind the ball and it only moves an inch or so, you *chili-dipped* it, partner. When your opponent does the same, you can rub it in by asking him, "You want a little chili with that dip?"

chip A *chip* is a short shot played near the green, the idea being to get the ball very near the hole. A *chip* is a shot played with the intention of the ball running quite a bit once it lands on the green. Because of this, a chip is differentiated from a pitch by these characteristics: The clubhead moves slightly back and through on a chip, but it moves almost halfway back and through on a pitch. You don't follow through at all on a chip, but you do on a pitch. A chip has a low or medium trajectory but would never be

described as a lofted shot. A chip doesn't usually bite (see *bite*)—when it does, it's an accident or the result of an expert player's attempt to make it do so. Pitches are played with the intention of the ball landing softly and rolling very little.

chip-and-run This is one of golf's more redundant terms because all chips are meant to run. So you'd never use this term if you want to sound like a real golfer; instead you'd simply say "chip." A *pitch-and-run* and a *bump-and-run* are other matters. They are specialty shots the names of which have good reasons for existing.

chip-in If you play a chip shot and it goes in the hole, it's a *chip-in*.

chipper When your buddies sit around talking about your ability as it relates to chipping, they would say you are a great *chipper*. (Well, you are, aren't you?)

The other use for this term is a club designed for the lone purpose of playing chip shots. If you want to be considered a real golfer by your friends, you best not have a *chipper* in your bag. And, fact is, you're making a public statement about your mental capacity if you carry a chipper since it

UPI/CORBIS-BETTMANN

Ray Floyd chips onto the green.

has the same loft as your seven-iron. If someone gives you a chipper as a gift (your secretary or your Uncle Elmo, who is a bowler), thank them profusely and place it, permanently, in the garage.

choke We've all done it. You're under pressure and you collapse for no reason other than the fact that you're under pressure. Well, you *choked*. And having done so, you're a *choker*. If you do it frequently, you've elevated yourself to the position of *choke artist*. The source of the pressure for a choker typically comes from within. When a player looks to place blame elsewhere, you know you're dealing with a choke artist.

choke down or **choke up** Whether you *choke down* or *choke up*, you're holding the club with your hands placed lower than the top of the club. It makes more sense to say you choke down because you are lowering your hands on the club and, in golf, the club is at a downward angle. However, some prefer to say choke up because that's the baseball term for when you move your hands away from the base of the bat's handle. In baseball, you always choke up because you hold the bat upright.

chunk When you stick the club into the ground too far behind the ball and, as a result, it flies less than the optimum distance, you've *chunked* it.

Church Pews A group of bunkers separating the third and fourth holes at Oakmont Country Club in Oakmont (a suburb of Pittsburgh), Pennsylvania, so called because the bunkers have horizontal rows of raised turf in the midst of them, which, collectively, resemble church pews.

Cinderella story In the movie *Caddyshack*, Bill Murray's character, Carl the Greenkeeper, holes out an imaginary shot to win the Masters (while chopping his way through a flower bed with a sickle) and imitates the announcers describing him as "a hometown boy, tear in his eye, a real *Cinderella story*." If you don't know who Cinderella is, you really ought to get out more.

claret jug, the You know that dream you always have, the one where you're standing on the steps of the R & A clubhouse in St. Andrews and some guy in a blue blazer and a soup-stained tie hands you the trophy for being British Open champion? That trophy is known as *the claret jug*. It's not just a claret jug, mind you, it's *the claret jug*.

claw grip The profusion of long putters on the Senior Tour beginning in the mid-1980s (see *long putter* and *Senior PGA Tour*) led to several new ways of gripping the club. One method, the *claw grip*, places the second and third finger on opposite sides of the shaft in a position that resembles the claw on a hammer.

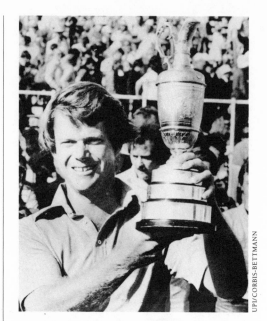

Tom Watson holds the claret jug aloft after his 1977 British Open victory.

clear the left side When you hear someone say that a golfer *clears his left side*, it simply means he turns completely through the ball at impact.

cleats Some players refer to their golf shoes as *cleats*, a reference to the metal spikes attached to the bottom of the shoes.

cleek This term is dated, so you'd never use it. Besides, it's confusing. A cleek was either a narrow-bladed iron, a one-iron, a four-wood, or a three-wood, depending on exactly which cleek you meant.

cleekmaker A person who made cleeks. He probably went out of business because no one knew what the hell he was selling.

click When you hit one perfectly, that sound and feel it makes is the *click*. Purists yearn for the click of persimmon against balata. When you start to play well, when you're really on a roll, you are *clicking* or things are starting *to click* for you.

clip A well-struck long iron shot from the fairway is said to be *clipped*, because the lead edge of the iron shears the grass without taking a divot. When you strike the shot, you *clip* it.

clone Golf equipment has become a big business, growing right along with the number of people playing the game. It's not surprising that many unscrupulous businesspeople counterfeit the most popular designs and sell them cheaper than the original manufacturer. Such clubs are called *clones* and generally lack the quality of the originals.

closed Your stance is *closed* if your left foot is closer to the target line than your right foot. Your clubface is *closed* if it is aimed left of the target at either address or impact.

closest-to-the-pin In many golf outings, a prize is awarded for the player who hits the ball closest to the hole on a designated par three. Such a contest is called a *closest-to-the-pin* contest.

club The *club* is the thing you strike the ball with. It has three parts: the grip, the shaft, and the clubhead.

When you ask your caddie which club you should use for a particular shot, you are asking him to *club* you. When he does so, he is *clubbing* you.

The *club* is also where you say you were in the event you belong to a private club and someone asks you what you did yesterday. "I went to the club," you say. "Oh, how nice," they say.

club champion At almost all golf clubs, both private and public, a championship is conducted annually to determine the best player in the club. Such an event is called the *club championship*, and the winner is the *club champion*. Formats vary from club to club.

clubface The part of the clubhead that is designed to make contact with the ball—at least on most shots. It's the part with the grooves on it, with the exception of the putter, which typically has no grooves. An expert player may occasionally play a shot that contacts a part of the clubhead other than the *clubface*, but these circumstances are rare. Chances are that you make contact with an area other than the clubface every so often—just don't brag about it.

clubhead The part of the club attached to the end of the shaft, designed and weighted to hit the ball various distances and at various trajectories.

clubhead speed The speed, in miles per hour, that the clubhead is moving at impact is known as *clubhead speed*. It is the major determining factor in creating distance.

club length Often, when you are entitled to relief, the Rules of Golf tell you to drop within one or two *club lengths* of the spot where the ball lay. A *club length* is the length of any club in your bag. Typically, a player will select the driver because it is the longest club.

clubmaker An individual who makes golf clubs.

club pro The golf professional (see *golf professional*) at a given club is sometimes referred to as the *club pro* or, simply, *the pro*.

cock In the backswing, the wrists cock, or bend toward the sky, when the clubhead starts to move upward. The wrists need to cock to allow the swing to reach its proper length.

coil During your backswing when your upper body turns around the resistance of your lower body, you are creating *coil*. Swingologists speak reverently of coil, for it is the source of power which, when unleashed in the downswing, results in a terrifying collision of clubface and ball at impact. Do yourself a favor and only use this term if you want to sound like a geek or, worse, television analyst Peter Kostis.

collar An alternative term for fringe or apron, it describes the closely mown grass that directly surrounds a green. The grass is approximately fairway height and separates the green from the rough.

collection area Some greens are designed so that, from certain portions of the green, all shots that roll off the green funnel to a common area known as a *collection area*. The collection area is meant to test the player's skill as a chipper or pitcher, since they will have to negotiate the slope their ball just rolled down in order to get close to the hole.

come back Something you would utter as you beg your ball to stop after an overzealous putt, chip, or bunker shot, as in, "Oh, *come back*. Please *come back*!"

comebacker When you make an aggressive run at a putt and miss, sending it well past the hole, the putt you have remaining is the *comebacker*. Most often, a comebacker is a par putt, left after an overly aggressive try for a birdie. In his heyday, Tom Watson was the king of the comebacker, making them without seeming to give it much thought. At the height of his major championship career, this was consistently pointed to as the strength of Watson's game.

come up If you're on the green and you're away and your buddy is in a bunker, you might wave to him and say, "*Come up*," indicating you wish him to play first in order to speed up play or simply as a courtesy.

component club This is a modern term that describes a club assembled by an individual as a hobby or as a small business enterprise. The clubs are called *component clubs* because the assembler purchases the elements of the club (grip, shaft, and clubhead) as individual components, typically from a mail order catalog or directly from one of several companies that distribute components. The advantage to this type of club is purely a matter of economics. Component clubs are significantly cheaper than clubs produced by the major club manufacturers.

compression Nowadays you don't hear much about the *compression* of a golf ball, since most players use two-piece golf balls and the manufacturers usually don't measure the compression of two-piece balls. However, balata balls are still sold according to their compression, designated by a number (typically 90 or 100) that indicates the amount the ball flattens at impact.

concede In match play, when you give someone a putt, that is to say, when you allow them to pick the ball up without holing out, you are *conceding* that putt. Typically, however, you would say, "That's good," or "Pick it up," to indicate you were willing to concede the putt. You may also *concede* a hole by picking up your own ball when it appears that your opponent is clearly going to win the hole. You might do this if he has a two-foot birdie putt on a par three and you've just whiffed for the eighth time in the greenside bunker.

connected A swingology term coined by noted teaching professional Jimmy Ballard (see *teaching professional*), *connected* refers to the idea of the upper left arm staying very close to the upper body in the backswing.

corded grip Some rubber grips are manufactured with bits and pieces of cord in them, which serve to make the surface of the grip more abrasive or rough than that of a smooth rubber grip, a feeling preferred by some players.

country club Some private golf clubs are referred to as *country clubs*, from the time when clubs were a weekend retreat for horse riding, hunting, and other pursuits of the wealthy. The modern country club might have such things as a golf course, tennis facilities, swimming pools, and other recreational facilities, as well as one or more dining rooms.

couple A long, long time ago when golfers played with tree branches, a partnership of two golfers was called a *couple*. Today, you'd probably get punched if you asked somebody to couple with you. You'd be better off just asking them if they'd like to be your partner.

course The *course* is the playing field for golf, a group of holes that usually total up to eighteen.

course management A player's ability to play a golf course in a manner that utilizes the player's strengths and downplays his weaknesses is his *course management*. Another way of putting it might be that a player who has excellent course management does not bite off more than he can chew.

course rat A golfer who seems to spend an inordinate amount of time playing golf is sometimes referred to as a *course rat*.

course rating A number assigned to every golf course that provides some indication of the course's difficulty.

course record The lowest score ever shot on a given course from the championship tees (see *championship tees*) is the *course record* for that course. If you want to act like you're a better player than you actually are, show up at a course you've never played before and inquire, "Where's the first tee and what's the course record?"

course setup A course's setup refers to the overall characteristics that influence the playability of a course other than its design. In other words, the length of the rough, the width at which the fairways are cut, the speed of the greens, and so forth, are all part of the *course setup*.

cow pasture If you think a golf course is a lousy course, you can call it a *cow pasture*. When you say this, you mean the ground would have been better utilized as a grazing pasture for bovine creatures.

creative shotmaking Some people see the glass as half empty; some people see it as half full. In golf, some people arrive at their ball and see only one possible shot; others arrive and see multiple ways of playing the next shot. The idea that you see many ways of playing your next shot is called *creative shotmaking*.

croquet-style putting This is now an illegal style of putting, but it was popularized by Sam Snead when he was having trouble on the putting greens.

Snead would straddle the line of the putt with the ball between his legs. He would place his left hand at the top of the grip and his right hand well down the shaft, almost near the head. The result was that he shoved the putt directly on the line he had chosen. After *croquet-style putting* was deemed illegal, Snead switched to a method where he stood with his body facing the hole and the ball off to the side of his right foot. He still gripped well down on the putter with his right hand, but it was not as effective as his original method.

cross bunker A bunker that crosses a fairway, perpendicular to the line of play.

cross-handed A style of gripping the club that puts the hands in a position opposite of that which is considered conventional. So a right-handed player, who typically places the right hand underneath the left hand, would place the right hand on top of the left. If you stumble upon a *cross-handed* player at your local course, be wary of thinking you've found yourself an easy mark. There's a good chance he's an excellent player and a better chance he's a self-taught hustler—and he's eyeballing you as the pigeon.

crunched A shot that is hit very hard and far is said to be *crunched*.

cup Slang for the hole.

cup liner The *cup liner* is typically made of plastic or metal and fits snugly inside the hole. Its purpose is twofold: to help the hole retain its shape and to provide a sturdy base for the flagstick (see *flagstick*). One of golf's more impromptu comedic moments is when the flagstick gets stuck in the cup liner while someone is tending the flag and, in desperation, the person yanks so hard on the flagstick that the liner is lifted out of the hole still attached to the flagstick.

cupped At the top of their backswing, many golfers seek to have their left wrist flat, with the top of the hand facing the sky. If you fail to achieve this position and your wrist is bent so that the top of the hand is facing the back of your head, the wrist is said to be *cupped*. Hopefully, you've got better things to worry about than whether or not your wrist is cupped at the top.

cuppy If your ball is sitting down in a bit of a hole or a depression in the ground, you have a *cuppy* lie.

curler A *curler* is a putt that breaks severely, sometimes in two different directions. Typically, the term *curler* is used in tandem with the word *long*, as in *long curler*. To sound like real golfer, you probably shouldn't refer to a short putt as a curler. Opt instead to call a short, hard-breaking putt a *slider*.

Curtis Cup A biennial team competition between women amateur players representing the United States, Great Britain, and Ireland.

customer golf One of golf's great attractions is that it is an appealing way of entertaining business clients. Of course, any good businessperson knows that you'd never want to beat a client or potential client. The act of playing down to a level that makes your client feel comfortable is known as *customer golf*.

cut This term has many uses within the game. When you hit a shot from left to right, that's a *cut* shot, but a real golfer would just say he *cut it*. Also, you might hear a player on television say he hit a little *cut* shot, and in that sense he's talking about a shot he hit from left to right, typically with a short iron, that had a little action on it when it hit the green (see *action*). Some golfers incorrectly refer to a high pitch shot played near the green as a cut shot, probably because the swing action in playing such a shot cuts underneath the ball. A real player would call this shot a flop shot, however.

If you still play a balata ball and you happen to catch a shot with the lead edge of an iron, you might put a *cut* in the ball.

In tournament play, the field of players is narrowed down, typically after two rounds, by the establishment of a cutoff number. The *cut* is said to be at that number. A player who equals or betters that number is said to have made the cut, while a player who fails to match that number is said to have missed the cut.

cutoff number The *cutoff number* is set after two rounds of tournament play. The number is different for every tournament played, and the basis for establishing that number varies from event to event. In professional play, you have to equal or better the cutoff number to make it to the final rounds and finish in the money.

cut the corner On any dogleg hole (see *dogleg*), a tee shot that you play with the intention of flying the ball over the curve in the fairway (rather than playing the hole straight away) is an attempt to *cut the corner*.

Cypress Point Golf Club Pebble Beach's next-door neighbor and one of the most exclusive golf clubs in the entire world, the Cypress Point Golf Club is best known for its sixteenth hole—probably the most photographed par three on the planet. At 216 yards with a 200-yard carry (see *carry*) over a finger of the Pacific Ocean, the green is surrounded by five bunkers. As a whole, the course may be the most beautiful course in the world.

The Cypress Point Golf Club is so exclusive that it was once the butt of this Bob Hope joke: "One year Cypress Point had a membership drive—they drove out forty members."

D

dance floor, on the This expression indicates that a shot you've hit has landed on the green but not quite as close as you would have liked it. Let's say you push a seven-iron just a tad, and your shot lands on the right side of the green while the hole is positioned on the left. In response to the mild torrent of expletives you unleash, one of your pals might say, "Lighten up, Herb, at least you're *on the dance floor*." The proper comeback to this is: "I might be on the dance floor, but I can't hear the band from over there."

dance with the one you brung with you You're on the fourth tee and you've hit a fade on every shot you've attempted on the first three holes (see *fade*). You don't particularly like to fade the ball, but it seems that's the way it's going to be on this particular day, so you make up your mind that for the rest of the round, you'll play for

Although these players still face challenging putts, they're at least on the dance floor.

STAN BADZ/PGA TOUR

the fade instead of fighting it all day. You've decided to *dance with the one you brung with you*, which is the saying pros use to describe just such a scenario. They use it because they know that things don't always go the way you plan in golf, so you have to adapt quickly.

dancing Slang for a ball that has a lot of action on it when it hits the green (see *action*). You're partner might say, "Man, that sucker was dancing!" To which you should nod approvingly.

dancing, you're Short for you're on the dance floor (see *dance floor, on the*).

dawn patrol The first few groups off the tee on any given morning at any given course are the *dawn patrol*. The term refers to the early morning patrols by infantry and air units in war.

dead If you hit the ball so close to the hole that even you can't miss the putt, you've hit it *dead*. If you hit the ball under a Stinging Death Ray tree and you're only option is to chip it back out to the fairway, you're *dead*.

dead-wristed Some short chip shots around the green are played with a stiff-armed stroke, without cocking the wrists. Such a stroke is *dead-wristed*.

decelerate When you putt, the idea is to keep the putter moving through the ball at a consistent speed. Sometimes, however, a player slows down the clubhead due to uncertainty. When you slow down the motion of the club in this manner, you are *decelerating* the club, which typically causes it to twist. That's not good.

deep When the hole is cut in the back of the green, you'll sound like a real player if you say, "The pin is *deep*."

deep-faced If the face of one of your clubs, particularly one of your woods, is long (or tall) from the lead edge to the top line of the club, it would be described as being *deep-faced* or, simply, *deep*.

delayed hit When the wrists stay fully cocked until very late in the downswing, it's sometimes referred to as a *delayed hit*. It's a silly term, since there's is nothing delayed about a delayed hit—it's actually a perfectly timed swing.

descending blow A *descending blow* is an image that a golf teacher would give you so that you would hit down on the ball, instead of scooping up at the ball. The truth of the matter is that nearly every full shot is struck with a descending blow; it just doesn't always feel that way.

desert course A golf course that is laid out over desert terrain is referred to as a *desert course*.

desert golf This term applies to circumstances you would encounter if you were playing on a desert course, specifically the fact that this type of course basically consists of tee boxes, fairways, and greens. Everything else is desert terrain, right down to the sand, rocks, cacti, snakes, and lots of other not-so-fun stuff.

desert rules On an off day, desert golf can get to be a bit brutal—balls flying into the desert left and right, endless searches for said balls. As such, those who frequently play in the desert play *desert rules*, which basically allow you to take a one-shot penalty and a drop at the point where your ball entered the desert, instead of playing it as a lost ball, which carries both a stroke and distance penalty.

deuce This is a term you want to use a lot, both because it will make you sound cool and because you'll have to be playing well to use it. A *deuce* is a two (birdie) on a par three, or a two on any other hole for that matter. Also,

after you hit that awesome two-iron shot that lands ten feet from the hole and your buddies ask you what you hit, you just say, "*Deuce*," and grab your putter from the bag.

Devil's Asshole Possibly the nastiest bunker in the entire world, the *Devil's Asshole* is a deep pit that fronts the par-three tenth hole at Pine Valley Golf Club, in Clementon, New Jersey. The bunker is so narrow that it's nearly impossible to take the club back in any direction without hitting the walls of the bunker.

dew sweeper When you rise with the sun in the morning and your group is among the first off the tee, you're a *dew sweeper*.

die When a ball *dies* on the putting green, it just runs out of gas on its way to the hole. Sometimes when you have a very fast downhill putt, you might try to *die* the ball at the edge of the hole in the hope that it might trickle into the hole.

Diegeling Want to try a putting stance that will make you look like a contortionist, try *Diegeling*, the name given to the bizarre manner of putting used by 1928 and 1929 PGA Championship winner Leo Diegel.

When Diegel was *Diegeling*, his elbows were pointed in extreme opposite directions—the left directly at the target, the right directly away from the target—and his forearms were horizontally parallel with the ground.

digger A player who takes a substantial divot with his iron shots is sometimes referred to as a *digger* since he digs into the ground with his club. The opposite of a digger is a picker (see *picker*).

dimple The little depressions on your golf ball are called *dimples*, and they help lift the ball into the air.

dimple pattern In the research and development departments of golf ball manufacturers, people sit in dark rooms surrounded by computers and concoct various ways to arrange the dimples on the cover of a golf ball. These arrangements are called *dimple patterns*, and somebody actually gets paid to figure them out.

dip If you have a *dip* in your swing, it just means you lower yourself to the ball a little bit through impact. Don't sweat it, it's no big deal. Also, if your ball goes in a water hazard, you might say it went for *a dip*, which would give you cause to *dip* into your pocket for another ball.

directional flag On holes where it is difficult to see the landing area, some courses elect to put a flag in the target zone that can be seen from the tee. Such a flag is known as a *directional flag*.

divot That big piece of turf you rip out of the ground on some of your iron shots is a *divot*. The hole you make in the ground is a *divot,* too. The word is derived from a Scottish word for the pieces of sod used to make roofs or, when dried out, used as fuel for fires. Whatever you do, don't call your pitch mark on the green a divot, and don't take a divot with your driver.

dogleg A hole that plays straight away from the tee and then veers sharply in one direction or another. A hole that bends to the right is called a *dogleg right*, and a hole that bends to the left is called a *dogleg left*.

dog track If you play a course that's rundown, unkempt, and not very difficult, tell your buddies it was a real *dog track*. You can also jokingly refer to a great course as a dog track, since people will know you're kidding, i.e., "That Augusta National is a dog track."

dormie In match play when you're ahead by as many holes as there are holes remaining to be played, you have your opponent *dormie*.

double Short for double bogey. You'll sound much cooler if you just say you made *double*. Just hope you don't have to sound cool in this manner too frequently.

double bogey A score of two more than par on a given hole.

double breaker A putt that curves in two different directions is a *double breaker*.

Double Chen In the 1985 U.S. Open, T. C. Chen of Taiwan was leading by a large margin on the final day. Leading, that is, until he double hit a pitch shot from the deep open rough midway through the round. The club contacted the ball, getting it airborne, and then

A double hit became a Double Chen after T.C. Chen's infamous shot at the 1985 U.S. Open.

AP/WIDE WORLD PHOTOS

hit the ball again. Since that day, some players refer to a double hit as a *Double Chen*, a play on the phrase *double chin*.

double cross When you set up to play a fade and instead you hit a hook, that's a *double cross*, and you've got big problems since you were aiming left and hit it even farther left. Same goes if you're planning on a draw and you hit a fade.

double dip This is music to any golfer's ears. When you and your partner both birdie the same hole, it's a *double dip*—double dip into your opponents' wallets, that is.

double eagle Probably rarer than a hole in one, a *double eagle* is a score of three strokes under par for a hole. The Brits refer to a double eagle as an albatross. The most famous double eagle of them all was Gene Sarazen's at the 1935 Masters (see *albatross*).

double green As with many things in the game, the idea of a double green comes from the Old Course (see *Old Course*). A *double green* is a giant putting green with two hole positions on it, which serves as the green for two separate holes.

double hit With the definite exception of a whiff and the possible exception of a shank (see *shank*), this is the most embarrassing shot in the game. A *double hit* occurs on pitches and chips when, after initial contact is made with the ball, the club momentarily sticks in the ground then pulls free, hitting the ball again while it's airborne. Oops.

doubles When a caddie carries the bags of two golfers at the same time, he's carrying *doubles*. A caddie who does so is referred to as a *doubles caddie*. Typically, a doubles caddie will sling one bag on each shoulder, but some choose to carry both on the same shoulder.

double sandy If you hit your drive in a fairway bunker, and then get up and down (see *up and down*) from a greenside bunker to make par, you've made a *double sandy*.

down On those rare occasions when you're behind in a match, you're *down*. If you trail by one hole, you're *one down*; two holes, you're *two down*, and so forth.

When you're attempting to get the ball in the hole, you're attempting to get it *down*. So, as your standing beside the eighteenth at Muirfield in the final round of the British Open and need only to hole out in two shots for a victory, Peter Alliss might say, "If he can just get down in two, he'll be Open champion." Having done so, you'll have gotten up and down (see *up and down*).

A few months earlier when you were in contention to win the U.S. Open and hit an errant drive into the rough, which nestled deep in the grass, Alliss might have said, "His ball appears to be sitting *down* in the grass." It's possible that your ball can be sitting down in the fairway, but it doesn't happen too often. If it is, it's either in an old divot or a small depression in the ground.

In the event that you and the others in your group decide to play a match wherein no one will improve their lie, you would say you are playing them *down*—"them" referring to the golf balls.

down and dirty On certain occasions, due to less than perfect course conditions or to the fact that some don't care to play by the Rules of Golf, players will decide to improve their lies as they see fit. If you don't care for this practice, you would inform your playing companions that you wish to play it *down and dirty*, a cool way of saying, "Play it as it lies."

downhiller If you're facing a putt that will run downhill, it's a *downhiller*. That's the only time you would use this term. Don't use it to refer to a downhill lie in the fairway—that's simply a downhill lie.

downhill lie A ball in a position which forces you to stand with your body leaning toward the target is considered a *downhill lie*.

downswing The part of your golf swing that begins at the end of your backswing and ends at impact with the ball. The beginning part isn't so clear, however, since the lower body starts its move down (turn forward) before the club has finished going back.

down the line This is one of those swingology terms you have no way of checking so you really shouldn't worry about it. In any case, your swing is said to be *down the line* when the club at the top is parallel to the target line and in line with your key body points—your feet, knees, hips, and shoulders. It's just a fancy way of saying your swing is on plane, and it's one of those things that makes sense only in golf because the club isn't actually pointing directly down the line. But, hey, if this stuff made sense, teachers wouldn't have to give many lessons.

down the road When you're playing in a tournament and you fail to qualify for the final rounds of play (you missed the cut), the caddies will say you're *down the road*. "The road" in this case is the driveway that leads into the club.

downtown When you crush one from the tee—just flat nail it—you've sent one *downtown*. Way to go, Crusher.

DQ There are a lot of rules in golf. Sometimes in tournament play when you don't comply with certain ones, you are disqualified from the competition. When this happens, you've been *DQ'd*, pal, and that's exactly what it will say next to your name in the newspaper.

drain it Sometimes a long, long putt unexpectedly goes in the hole. When that happens you've *drained* it, just like water down a drain.

draino This is what you yell as you're jumping up and down on the green after you drain one. Or after the round when you're thrilling your drinking partners with the tale of that epic putt, you might say: "There I was on the thirteenth with a 90-footer for birdie and bam! Draino!"

draw A controlled shot that moves from right to left in the air.

dribbler When all is said and done, you'd rather dribble a basketball or dribble milk down your chin than hit a dribbler on the golf course. A *dribbler* moves just a few inches after a near whiff.

drink Hit your ball in a water hazard, and you're in *the drink*. The term is borrowed from World War II aviators, who referred to the ocean as the drink.

Approach shots at Colonial Country Club's sixteenth often wind up in the drink.

drive Pay attention here because this is an important one if you want to sound like a real golfer. On any par four or par five, the shot you play from the tee is your *drive*, no matter what club you hit. On a par three, you never hit a drive, even if you use your driver. On a par three, you hit a tee shot.

Back in olden days when you played from the first tee, you were said to *drive off*, but only on the first tee because it referred to the fact that the match was off and, presumably, running. And on that magical day when you are made captain of the Royal and Ancient Golf Club of St. Andrews, you will hit a ceremonial shot from the first tee and *drive* yourself into office. Congratulations.

drive and a pitch Short par-four holes are frequently referred to as *drive-and-a-pitch* holes because a solid drive and a simple pitch shot will put the player safely on the green.

drive for show, putt for dough This overused but ever accurate saying refers to the fact that the hole isn't over simply because one player hits an impressive drive. There aren't any fat ladies singing in golf, but this is the equivalent. In a hotly contested match, the holes are usually decided on the greens, where you *putt for dough*.

driver Theoretically, this is the longest club with the least amount of loft in your set, designed for playing the ball from the tee. Let's get this straight right off the bat, however: Never, ever refer

DENNIS ROBERSON

58

to your *driver* as your number one wood, even though it has the numeral one stamped on the bottom of it. Call it a big gun, a big stick, a cannon, anything you want—just don't call it the one-wood.

There was a time when the *driver* had standard lengths and lofts, but those days are long gone. Gone, too, are the days when the driver was designed to be played only from a tee, since modern metal designs have made it possible and practical to play the clubs off the ground.

When your friends whisper in hushed tones about how well you hit the ball from the tee, they say you're a great *driver*.

driving area The area on a hole intended by the architect to receive tee shots is known as the *driving area*.

driving iron, driving mashie, driving putter These are all clubs that haven't been used since the days when golfers had to sneak out of church to tee up. Even though you're deadly with your one-iron, do not refer to it as your *driving iron*. Please. The *driving putter* was a long-nosed wooden club used to play low, powerful shots into the wind about the time Abe Lincoln was president.

driving range *Driving ranges* used to be places you took your date to impress her with your ability to whack drives prodigious distances or smack the side of the old station wagon that was driving around the range (a big open field) at five miles per hour. Wooden slats separated the teeing areas, which were covered with green carpet and had a rubber tee protruding about three inches above the carpet. You received your balls in wire buckets (small, medium, or large) and beat on them with a laminated wooden driver you picked off a rack.

Today, *driving ranges* have prettied themselves up a bit and the proprietors prefer to call them practice ranges or golf centers. It's amazing, but golfers now go to these places for serious practice. When you do so and someone asks where you were, just say, "At the range."

drop The primary meaning of this term refers to what you sometimes do when you incur a penalty or when you are entitled to relief. When you *drop* a ball, you are doing just that—dropping it. Anytime the Rules of Golf dictate that you *drop* (when you declare a ball unplayable, hit one in the water or take relief), you do so by extending your arm directly in front of you and letting go of the ball. Where you drop the ball depends on the circumstances.

Also, when a putt falls into the hole, it is said to *drop*. After a round, you might tell your wife, who is no doubt hanging on your every word, that you dropped a long one at the ninth.

In medal play, when you make a bogey (or worse), you have *dropped* a stroke or strokes to par.

dropkick Here's a clue that will help you sound like a real golfer. You can only hit a dropkick with a wood. What is it? When you hit a shot and the wood feels as if it bounces off the ground and then hits the ball, that's a *dropkick*. Actually, the result is usually not too horrible. You can only hit a dropkick with a wood because of the shape of the bottom of the club. If you made the same swing with an iron, you'd take a divot deep enough to serve as a wine cellar.

drop like a cat A ball that hits the green and stops quickly is sometimes said to *drop like a cat*, the allusion being that the ball looked like it had claws.

dual wedge This is another of those clubs in the same family as the chip-per (see *chipper*). Its reason for existing is to provide guys who throw nickels around like manhole covers an, er, inexpensive alternative to purchasing a pitching wedge and a sand wedge. The fact is, partner, the same club can't do double duty. You're a true golfer, so if you have a *dual wedge*, give it to the kids.

dub A *dub* is a good way to describe nearly any (lousy) shot that moves only a few feet or yards.

dubber If people frequently refer to you as a *dubber*, you either need to practice more or drop golf in favor of model airplanes because you stink.

duck hook A hook is a shot that curves sharply from right to left. A *duck hook* is a shot that appears to have been shot out of the sky by a skeet shooter, airborne one second, plummeting to earth the next. It's an ugly shot, so called because the ball appears to duck to the ground in a hurry—and so do the people playing with you. The good news is there's no such thing as a duck slice.

dues *Dues* are the fees a person pays to belong to a private golf or country club. In a metaphorical sense, *paying your dues* refers to a player who practices hard and experiences failure and setbacks before finally achieving success.

duff Aside from being the name of the excellent beer sucked down by Homer Simpson and his buddies at Moe's Bar, a *duff* is yet another way of referring to an extraordinarily poor shot. After the fact, you would say you *duffed* it.

duffer If you're a *duffer*, you're going to suffer—and so is the golf course. Face it, friend, you're not good. Not even a little bit.

dunch An old (really old) Scottish term for the act of striking a low, forceful, running shot. The shot itself is called a *dunced* shot, and you'll sound like a dunce if you use this term. Opt instead for *punch* or *bump*.

E

eagle A score of two under par on a hole.

effective loft The *effective loft* of a club is the actual angle of the clubface at impact, as opposed to the amount of loft built into the club. In other words, if your swing or ball position (see *ball position*) places the club in a position that alters the true loft of the club, the actual amount of loft is referred to as effective loft.

egg Want to sound like an old-time touring pro? Next time you have a good putting round tell your friends you had a good day rolling the egg. Don't refer to your ball as an *egg* under any other circumstances. There is a *fried egg*, but that refers to a lie in a bunker, not specifically to the ball.

eight-iron An iron with approximately 41 to 44 degrees of loft and a lie of 62 to 63 degrees. When clubs went by names instead of numbers, an *eight-iron* was known as a pitching niblick.

eighteen The number of holes on a regulation golf course. If you say to someone, "I managed to get in a quick *eighteen* this morning," it means you played golf.

elephant burial ground When a green has a lot of severe undulations in it you might say, "Man, it's like putting over an *elephant burial ground*." The idea is that if you were to dig a hole to bury an elephant, you probably wouldn't dig it deep enough and when you covered it, there would be big humps of dirt. For some reason, no one ever says "elephant cemetery."

elephant's ass If you pop a shot straight up into the air, one of your pals might say, "That's an *elephant's ass*," the metaphor meaning that the shot was high and stinky.

elevated green An *elevated green* is one that is built up higher than the fairway or higher than the tee on a par three.

elevated tee An *elevated tee* is one that is significantly higher than the general terrain. Many tees are slightly higher than the overall terrain, so you have to be up there a bit to call it an elevated tee.

embedded ball Any ball that gets stuck in the ground upon landing is an *embedded ball*. If your ball becomes embedded in the fairway, fringe, or any other closely mown area (fairway height or less), you can lift it, clean it, and drop it. If it becomes embedded in a hazard or in the rough, you're out of luck.

escape When your ball lands in a precarious position and you successfully manage to extricate yourself from this position, you have *escaped*. The shot you played to save the day was an *escape shot*.

equitable stroke control A manner of protecting against scores that will throw a player's handicap out of whack, *equitable stroke control* requires that players take no more than a certain score for a given hole. It's purely a handicapping apparatus.

etiquette Collectively, *etiquette* refers to the acts that result from a player being aware of and courteous to other players, while being certain to do his best not to destroy the golf course.

European PGA Tour The series of European events that make up the annual schedule of top-level competition for professional golfers.

SAM GREENWOOD/PGA TOUR

Nick Faldo was a longtime star of the European PGA Tour.

even When you shoot a score equivalent with par for a course, you've shot a round of *even* par. To sound like a real golfer, you'd simply say *even*. In response to the question, "What did you shoot today?" you would say calmly, "Oh, I was even." You would also say you were even if at any point during the round you were level with par up to that point.

If you're in a match play situation, you're *even* if neither you nor your opponent is leading the match.

even par You're at *even par* any time your total score matches par (see *par*), be it your round in progress (which would count par for only those holes you've played) or your total afterward.

executive course *Executive course* is a euphemism for a pitch-and-putt course, a layout of mostly par threes and a few extremely short par fours. Real golfers don't play *executive courses* or, in general, acknowledge their existence.

exempt Sometimes a player is *exempt* from qualifying for a tournament or series of events, typically because of past performance.

exemption An *exemption* in professional golf allows the player to whom it's awarded to compete in events without having to otherwise qualify for them. For example, a player who wins the Players Championship (see *Players Championship*) is awarded a 10-year exemption for the entire PGA Tour. Another example is the Masters, where all winners are granted an automatic *exemption* to all subsequent Masters Tournaments. Typically, on the professional tour, the sponsoring organization for a tournament is allowed to hand out a couple of *sponsor's exemp-*

tions as a token of appreciation for their financial generosity. This type of exemption basically allows them to invite any competitive player into the field.

explode When you *explode* from the sand, the gritty stuff flies all over the place, much more so than in a typical bunker shot. The shot, which is called an *explosion shot,* is played when the ball is buried in the sand or is very close to the lip (see *blast*).

extension This term refers to the idea that your arms should be fully stretched or fully extended at impact and just beyond impact.

extra holes When a match is even at the end of the prescribed number of holes for that match (18 or 36), the players go to *extra holes* to decide the outcome. First one to win a hole wins the match. In stroke play, this is called sudden death more frequently than extra holes.

F

face The part of the clubhead designed to contact the ball (see *club-face*). The angle of the *face* at impact affects the direction and trajectory of the ball in flight. On all clubs except the putter, the face is where the scoring lines (grooves) are located.

When you're in a bunker, the bank of grass or sand that is staring you in the face is also a *face*. It's the part of the bunker you need to clear (along with the bit of rough and the fringe) in order for your ball to reach the green.

fade An intentional shot that curves from left to right. The difference between a *fade* and a slice, which also curves from left to right, is that a slice curves significantly more and typically beyond a predictable amount (see *slice*). The word *fade* refers to both the shot in flight and the act of hitting the shot. The fade is generally regarded as a scoring shot—a shot over which the excellent player has maximum control.

When you're near the lead in stroke play competition (aren't you always?) but fail to keep pace down the stretch, you have *faded*. When you begin to slip out of the lead you are *starting to fade*, and when you continue to do so, you are *fading*.

fair green An obsolete term that corresponds approximately to the modern usage of *fairway*. *Fair green* referred to areas where the grass was short and free of hazards and other obstacles such as trees and bushes.

fairway The *fairway* is the closely mown area between the tee and green on par fours and par fives and is the preferred route for playing the hole. The term is borrowed from sailors, the nautical usage referring to a clear channel between rocks or shallows. If you want to sound like a real golfer, remember that par threes don't have fairways, at least in the sense that any closely mown area other than the green is intended as a landing area for a tee shot.

fairway bunker A hazard, either grass or sand, that is placed adjacent to or in a fairway. Depending upon the intentions of the course designer, a *fairway bunker* can serve as a hazard to be avoided or carried on the tee shot or simply as a clearly visible guidepost to the routing of the hole. In some cases, a fairway bunker is placed closer to the green, well out of range of the tee shot, to create depth deception on the approach or simply to snag weak approach shots.

fairways and greens A term used by tour players to describe their strategy on particularly difficult courses or under pressure-filled situations such as the final round of a tournament or any round in the U.S. Open. The term refers to the idea that by not getting too greedy—by focusing on placing tee shots anywhere in the fairway and approach shots anywhere on the green—the player stands an excellent chance of shooting a good score.

fairways hit A statistic that refers to the number of times a player's tee shots land in the fairway on driving holes. A measurement of accuracy, the number is used for a given round or tournament and as a percentage over the course of an entire professional tour season.

fairway wood Any of the wood clubs, other than the driver, designed for playing long shots from the fairway. Modern club design (particularly the design of the sole on metal woods) has made these clubs equally valuable (and realistic selections) for long shots from the rough. However, there is no term *rough wood*.

Faldo, Nick The dominant major championship performer (see *major* *championships*) from the late 1980s through this writing, Faldo has won three Masters and three British Opens and has contended in numerous other majors. Renowned as the most precise striker of the ball in his era, Faldo emerged from the pack as a result of hard work and a mind-set that some liken to that of Ben Hogan.

Fall Classic Tour player's slang for the PGA Tour Qualifying School, which is held each year in the fall (see *Q School*).

false green A course design element conceived by Alistair MacKenzie, main architect of Augusta National and Cypress Point (see *Augusta National Golf Club* and *Cypress Point Golf Club*). *False green* is a term for a steeply banked portion at the front of a green that allows a player, particularly on an uphill hole, to make visual contact with the green. However, any shot hitting this part of a green would simply roll off the green, hence it is *false*—the true green lies beyond.

fan A whiff, an air shot, the complete absence of contact between the clubhead and ball on an attempted shot. The term almost surely refers to the slight breeze created by the clubhead as it passes the ball. Similar in usage to the same term in baseball—a swing and a miss.

fast This term is used mainly to describe the condition of greens when the ball rolls extremely quickly along the putting surface. The term refers to the green itself (a *fast* green) and to individual putts (a *fast* putt). The speed of greens is determined by using a device called a stimpmeter (see *stimpmeter*). Less common is a usage that refers to an entire course as *playing fast*. Typically, this describes a course that plays over hard ground, causing the ball to run much more than normal once it hits the ground.

fat The act of the lead edge of the clubhead digging into the ground too far behind the ball. This is not a good thing. Typically, a *fat* shot occurs when the angle of clubhead into the ball is too steep and/or when the ball is positioned too far back in the stance.

The *fat part of the green* refers to the largest part of the putting surface that will accept and hold an approach shot. More often than not, this refers to the center of the green. A player under pressure or protecting a lead may choose not to play toward a difficult hole position (for example, one tucked behind a bunker) and opt to play for the fat of the green, presumably to avoid making a score worse than par.

feather This term describes a shot in which a player hits the ball with less than the full value of a given club while apparently making a full swing. A *feathered shot* is played by slowing down the speed of the swing and is executed for two reasons: to play a shot a certain distance with a lower trajectory and, mainly, to fool an opponent in match play. Since it is legal to look in a player's bag to see what club he has used for a certain shot, savvy match players sometimes take more club than necessary for a given shot and feather it to trick their opponents.

featherie The hand-sewn, leather ball used approximately from 1620 to 1850, before being replaced with the more durable gutta-percha ball. The *featherie* was so named because it was stuffed with feathers. The amount of feathers was equivalent to a top hat full. The feathers were then boiled and stuffed into a leather casing. The term also refers to the era in golf from 1620 to 1850 (the Featherie Era) during which the ball was used.

feel Perhaps the most ambiguous word in the game, it refers to an intuitive sense for playing the game and executing shots, which cannot be described using the mechanical terms ordinarily used for identifying the various parts or the whole of the golf swing. If you've got *feel*, you know it—you were born with it. If you don't have it, you never will.

feel player One who plays the game and the shots with an ethereal sense, as opposed to a player who concentrates on swing mechanics and exact yardages. You should take it as a compliment if someone calls you a *feel player*—unless you're in a cow pasture at the time.

feel shot A shot that requires a natural sense to execute or, in other words, a shot that cannot be taught or learned.

fellow competitor In stroke play competition, the player or players with whom a golfer is paired are his *fellow competitors*. A common error is to refer to fellow competitors as playing partners, but the players in a stroke play group are not partners.

ferrule The plastic cap that covers the part of the club where the shaft and the hosel are joined in some iron designs, typically forgings (see *shaft* and *hosel*). Purely cosmetic, *ferrules* are not used on many of today's cast club designs.

fescue Any grass of the genus *Festuca*, fescue grass is typically found on seaside links. Many of the courses in the British Isles have *fescue* fairways and greens, not to mention a mixture that includes fescue in the rough. Many believe closely cropped *fescue* to be the finest surface from which to play iron shots. If you watched any of the 1986 or 1995 U.S. Opens at Shinnecock Hills, you saw plenty of your favorite players hacking away in the native fescue at one of the few great American courses to have the stuff.

AP PHOTOCOLOR

The 1995 U.S. Open was played at Shinnecock Hills, one of the few U.S. courses to boast fescue grass.

fifteenth club An expression used to describe a state of mind that helps a player maintain composure under extreme pressure, i.e., patience or thoughts of an influential person or teacher. The term is based on the fact that fourteen is the maximum number of clubs allowed in competition and that a *fifteenth club* somehow provides an advantage unavailable to other players in the field. When Ben Crenshaw won the 1985 Masters just one week after his mentor Harvey Penick died, Crenshaw referred to his inspirational thoughts of Penick as a fifteenth club.

fighting If all of your poor shots during a given round are the same, you're said to be *fighting* that particular shot. For example, if you're slicing all of your tee shots, you're fighting a slice. If your game is lousy overall, you might say you're fighting your swing. Hot tip: The swing usually wins.

final pairing In tournament play, this is the last group to tee off in the final round. Typically, the players in this group are leading the tournament at the beginning of the final round.

find or **found** Used to describe the outcome of an errant shot that is about to land in or has landed in a hazard. "That shot is going to *find* trouble," or "He *found* the bunker with that shot."

finish An alternate term for the follow-through position. Your teacher might tell you, "Swing through to the *finish.*" *Finish* also refers to the ability of a player leading a tournament to successfully complete the final few holes and win the tournament, despite the pressure. Such a player is said to know how to f*inish*. A person who knows how to finish is a *great finisher*. If ever there was a great finisher, it was Jack Nicklaus, a man who won many big tournaments because he knew how to finish when the same could not be said of many of his contemporaries.

fire right at it Phrase used to indicate that a player intends to play a shot directly at the hole, particularly under circumstances where a safer line of play would seem prudent.

fire the right side A swing mechanics expression used to describe the action of the right hip initiating the downswing and turning rapidly toward the target. The idea of *firing the right side* can be seen in the extreme action of Gary Player, who actually steps through the ball with his right foot and leg on the follow-through.

firm Term used to describe the condition of fairways and greens when the ground is harder than normal. *Firm* fairways and greens are considered standard for championship play, placing a premium on accurate tee shots and approach shots.

firm left side A swing mechanics expression that describes a straight vertical line along the left side of the body at impact, with the left leg and left side of the torso braced for the collision at impact. A player who achieves this position is said to be hitting against a *firm left side*.

first on wins In match play, some players feel that the first player on the green normally wins the hole, thus the expression *first on wins*. Players who think this way often play for the fat of the green (see *fat*) rather than risk playing directly at the flagstick.

fit A person is *fit* for a set of clubs much the way he is fit for a suit. The length, lie, loft, and shaft flex of the club are chosen based on the person's physical attributes and swing mechanics.

A shot can be said to *fit* a hole when the player shapes the shot to take advantage of the terrain and the design of the hole. For example, on a hole that curves from right to left, a player would hit a draw to fit the shape of the hole. Among current tour players, Corey Pavin is the king of fitting shots to a hole.

A particular course can also be said to *fit* a player. For example, Augusta National favors players who draw the ball because many of the holes bend to the left. If you were playing at Augusta (yeehah!) and you played a draw as your preferred shot, the announcers would say something like, "Augusta National fits this young man's game nicely." (See that, not only are you playing in the Masters, but you're a young man to boot!)

five-iron An iron club with approximately 29 to 32 degrees of loft and 59 to 61 degrees of lie.

fivesome A group consisting of five players, which is one more than the standard nontournament grouping. If at any time you find yourself playing behind a *fivesome*, feel free to hit into them. They deserve it.

five-wood A wood club with approximately 21 to 23 degrees of loft and 55 to 56 degrees of lie.

flag A banner or pennant hung from a stick or pole that is placed in the

hole. Typically a bright color, the *flag* is intended to be an easily spotted indicator of the hole position.

flagged it To hit a shot very close to the hole, right at the flagstick. A good example of flagging it under pressure took place in the final round of the 1972 U.S. Open at Pebble Beach when Jack Nicklaus hit the flagstick with his tee shot at the par-three seventeenth hole.

flagstick A stick, pin, or pole with a flag (or other marker) attached to the top, the flagstick shows the position of a hole.

flame-broiled A real "whopper" of a drive, one that is hit extremely hard and far. Flame-broiled is also the way the fast-food chain Burger King advertises the cooking for its flagship sandwich, the Whopper.

flange On some iron clubs, a protrusion from the back of the club. Some putters have a *flange* for additional weight. On a sand wedge, the *flange* is the part of the club that causes the club to bounce off the sand rather than dig into it.

flat When your swing is *flat*, it means that the plane of it (the angle at which the club swings around your body) is low or close to the ground, much like Lee Trevino's (dream on, partner). Your backswing would be *flat*, but not your follow-through. Not that your follow-through couldn't be, mind you, it's just that no one refers to it as such.

What's the difference between flat, perfect, and upright? If you have a perfect address position, the angle of the shaft at address is roughly equal to the angle of a perfectly on-plane swing. Ben Hogan used the image of a pane of glass resting on the shoulders (there's a hole in the pane for your head to fit through) to illustrate the perfect swing plane. If your club dips below that plane, your swing is considered flat.

Your clubs have a quality known as lie (see *lie*), which describes the angle at which the shaft joins the club-head. If this angle is wider than standard for a given club, your clubs are considered *flat*.

When you play a course that is devoid of hills and undulation, you'd describe it as *flat*. The same goes for greens that don't have much undulation.

flatbellies An expression used by older tour players to refer to their younger and, typically, more physi-cally fit counterparts. Lee Trevino pop-ularized it, but it's difficult to say if he was the first to use it.

flatstick Slang term for a putter, it refers to the apparent lack of loft on most putters, though a typical putter has a few degrees of loft.

flex The amount that a clubshaft bends when swung. Shafts are designed and manufactured to *flex* var-ious amounts and at different points, depending upon the speed at which the club is swung and the amount of trajectory the player desires. When a club flexes in the backswing, it is said to be loading or storing up power. The shaft unloads in the downswing as the clubhead nears impact.

flick The action of the wrists and the resulting delicate chip shot in a situa-tion that requires the ball to be picked cleanly from a fluffy greenside lie. A *flick* shot is played when the ball is sit-ting atop the grass.

flier Both the lie and the resulting shot that occurs when the ball is sitting up in the rough. The shot is so named because it flies or carries farther than it typically would with a given club. The reason for this is that the long blades of grass get trapped between the clubface and the ball, eliminating the spin. In addition to extra carry, the lack of spin from a *flier* lie makes it difficult to stop the ball on the green. Some would argue that the advent of square (box-shaped) grooves has eliminated the latter condition, but this would typically apply only to the exceptional player.

flight A manner of categorizing players in club tournaments so that players of approximately the same skill level are matched against each other. The best players play in the championship *flight*, the next level is the A *flight,* and so on. The term also refers to the action of the ball while it is airborne on full shots.

flip shot. A short approach shot, typically played with a wedge and intended to land softly and roll to the hole. It's called a *flip shot* because the swing is less than full; the clubhead and ball are "flipped" toward the hole.

flip wedge A flip shot played with a wedge.

floater A ball designed to float in the water, in the hope that the striker of the ball might retrieve it.

flop shot A delicate shot that requires tremendous skill, the *flop shot* is usually attempted when the player must carry a bunker and the hole is cut close to the opposite side of that bunker. The shot, played with a sand wedge with the face laid completely open, flies extremely high and lands with little or no roll.

The shot requires a clean lie because the clubhead must be slipped under the ball. Although the ball flies only a few yards, the backswing and follow-through are the length of a full swing, and the club must be swung at a high speed. The result is that the ball pops almost straight into the air. The flop shot doesn't always have to be played over a bunker. Tom Watson's famous hole-out at Pebble Beach's seventeenth in the 1982 U.S. Open could be described as a modified flop shot. He didn't take a full swing at it, but it had the qualities of such a shot.

flub Any mis-hit shot. The term (in its nongolf sense) refers to the act of bungling an attempt to do just about anything.

fluff Yet another term for a mis-hit shot, its origins are the stage, where an actor who blew his part was said to have fluffed it.

fluffy lie A lie where the ball is sitting atop the grass, so there is a cushion of grass beneath the ball.

fly The distance a ball carries in the air. If you have to carry a bunker 180 yards away, you'd say, "I'll have to *fly* it 180 yards." After you've carried the bunker, you'd say you *flew* it 180 yards. Also, in a negative sense, a fly can refer to a shot that carries over the green without ever touching the putting surface. If you send one sailing clear over the green, you'd say, "I *flew* the green."

fly, on the The distance a ball carries without any roll, e.g., "I hit it 260 yards *on the fly*."

flying right elbow A swing mechanic's term used to describe a right elbow that does not stay close to the body, which generally accepted as conventional in a proper swing. While it is not considered typical, many great players, including Jack Nicklaus and Miller Barber, have had a *flying right elbow*.

fog A growth of moss or long grass. Almost exclusively Scottish in use, the term apparently has no relationship to fog in its traditional sense.

fold When your pal Slasher falls apart on the final few holes, you would say

STAN BADZ/PGA TOUR

Miller Barber's flying right elbow is apparent at the top of his swing.

he *folded*. Later on, when you're telling everyone what a choker he is, you would say, "He folded like a house of cards."

follow through, follow-through position *Follow through* on a shot refers to the act of continuing the swing to completion after contacting the ball. The *follow-through position* is the final position of the accepted mechanical stages of the golf swing.

foot wedge Slang for cheating by nudging or kicking the ball with one's foot.

foozle A poorly hit shot. A favorite of the great writer P. G. Wodehouse, the term was originally used by English schoolboys to describe someone who fooled around a lot. If you *foozle* often, you're a *foozler*. But at least Wodehouse would have loved you.

fore In essence, this means "Look out, you're about to get hit in the head with my shot!" Scottish in origin, it was meant to warn the group be*fore* (ahead of) you, but it's now used as a general warning to players anywhere on the course that an errant shot may be headed their way. If you hear this frequently where you play, look around for new home course.

forecaddie A caddie who stays ahead of the players to mark the lie of the balls in play. In its original Scottish use, it meant "before caddie." Today, it generally refers to a single caddie who goes out with a foursome of cart-riding golfers. The modern *forecaddie* carries the players' putters at all times, so players can exit their carts and proceed directly to the green. While the caddie is performing this service for the lazy slobs in the carts, he is *forecaddying*.

forged iron Irons that are hewn from a solid block of stainless steel. *Forged irons*, noted for their tremendous feel, are also noted for their lack of forgiveness on mis-hit shots. Forged irons are sometimes referred to as forged blades.

form Generally British in use, *form* refers to the standard of play for a golfer during a particular period of time, be it a single round, tournament, or sustained stretch of time. A player at the top of his game is said to be *on form* or in *good form*.

forward press In the full swing or with the putting stroke, the *forward press* is the movement of the hands and wrists toward the target to initiate the swing. The forward press feels quite natural to some players and is touted as a method for reducing tension.

forward tees On courses that have staggered tee boxes for players of various skill levels, these are the tees closest to the green.

four-ball A match between the best ball of two teams, each consisting of two players. (Also see *best ball*.)

four-iron An iron club having approximately 27 to 28 degrees of loft and 58 to 60 degrees of lie. In days gone by, the four-iron was known as a mashie.

four-jack A four-putt or four putts on a given hole.

four-putt To take four putts on a hole. Spaniard Seve Ballesteros, twice Masters champion, was once asked how he managed to *four-putt* a hole at Augusta National and responded: "I miss, I miss, I miss, I make."

fours, level A score that averages out to a four on each hole, or a 72 total.

foursome The standard nontournament grouping of four players.

foursomes A match between two teams, each consisting of two players playing a single ball by alternate strokes. This is one type of match played in the Ryder Cup.

fourth, a "Need a fourth?" That's what you'd ask someone if you hear a few guys are thinking about playing or if you approach a threesome on the first tee and would like to play along with them. What you mean is do they need *a fourth* player to round out their group.

four-whack A four-putt.

four-wood A wood club with approximately 18 to 20 degrees of loft and 55 to 57 degrees of lie. Formerly referred to as a spoon.

fried egg Slang for the lie of a ball half-buried in the sand, with the top half of the ball visible. Named for its resemblance to a sunny-side up egg.

frog hair A slang term for the fringe or apron around the green.

front, the Slang for the first nine holes of a golf course or the outward (away from the clubhouse) nine. To sound like a real golfer you might say, "I shot 43 on *the front* with two doubles." That is, you made two double bogeys.

front nine The first nine holes of a golf course.

front-runner A player noted for playing particularly well when he holds the lead in a tournament, distancing himself from the rest of the field. The term almost certainly is derived from horse racing and running races. Raymond Floyd was legendary for his ability as a *front-runner*—when he got out in front he was very difficult to catch.

Raymond Floyd, a legendary front-runner.

SAM GREENWOOD/PGA TOUR

frost delay In the early spring and late fall, a delay in the scheduled tee times might occur due to frost on the greens.

Frosty A slang term for a slang term. A score of eight on a single hole is referred to as a snowman because the numeral resembles a snowman. Frosty, of course, is the most famous snowman of all.

frozen rope From the baseball term for a line drive, a tee shot that is solidly hit but does not reach maximum trajectory.

full To hit a club its maximum distance, i.e., to hit a *full* seven-iron.

fungo A practice shot. When a player hits balls on the practice range, he is hitting fungos. The term is borrowed from baseball.

fuzzy greens Slang expression for greens that have not been mown to a height that allows the ball to roll properly. If you play a lot of golf at public courses, you know what *fuzzy greens* are like.

G

gag Another of the seemingly endless ways of describing a collapse under pressure. After you *gag*, you'd like to gag the guys you're playing with every time they remind you of it.

gallery Sometimes it seems like a good idea to spend a pleasant afternoon in the sun, watching some players who actually know what they are doing. If you choose to do this in Great Britain, you'd say you were going to *gallery* the match. If you did this in the United States, you would be watching the match as part of the *gallery*—the entire group of people watching the proceedings. While doing so, you

The gallery was packed.

STAN BADZ/PGA TOUR

might say you were *gallerying*—but you'd be better off just saying you watched or followed the play. As a member of the gallery, you would be ordained a *galleryite*, which means when a ball bounces off your head and ricochets onto the green, the television announcers will say, "Greg Norman got a luck bounce off a galleryite." Of course, if you were a member of golf's most famous gallery, that of Arnold Palmer (see *Arnie's Army*), you'd gladly throw yourself in front of any shot in the hope that it would bounce off you.

game Hopefully, you realize golf is a *game*—it's a good idea never to lose sight of that fact. Don't ever tell your wife or boss you're heading out for a game of golf, however, because no real golfer would use the word in that manner. You would sound like a real golfer if you use *game* for any of the following meanings:

If you called your buddy Jacques Nickluss on the phone to see if he wants to tee it up with you on Saturday, you would first inquire, "Do you have *a game* for Saturday?" This allows you to determine if Jacques was already planning to play prior to your call.

If you're standing on the first tee wondering whether or not anyone is in the mood for a little betting action, you can ask the boys, "Anyone up for a *little game*?" You should say *little game* no matter what size wager you're interested in making—especially if you want to play for some serious cash.

Once you've decided to play for some dough-ra-me, it's time to decide which type of betting will take place. This is when you say, "What *kind of game* are we going to play?"

Later in the day when you're emptying your wallet to the guy who beat your brains in, you can shake your head in despair and say in admiration, "Man, you've got *a lot of game.*"

game improvement club It's a given that your game is solid, but not everyone is quite so lucky. One of the big problems many golfers have is an inability to hit the ball with the center of the clubface. For a long time, any ball that contacted the toe or the heel of the club didn't have much power and didn't go very straight. *Game improvement clubs* changed all of that. In the early 1970s, an engineer named Karsten Solheim introduced a new concept to golf club design called perimeter weighting (see *perimeter-weighted irons*) in his company's Ping golf clubs. Perimeter weighting took weight from the center of the club and moved it to the outer edges of the club. The result was that mis-hit shots turned out a heck of a lot better than they did in the days when clubs were just a solid hunk of steel. This genre of clubs came to be known as game improvement clubs because they made the game much easier for the average player—and a lot more fun.

When metal woods were introduced into the golf mainstream, they too were classified as game improvement clubs.

gamesmanship This is one of the naughtiest words in golf. *Gamesmanship* doesn't refer to out-and-out cheating; rather it refers to an attempt to rattle your opponent by breaching the unwritten code of etiquette that is expected of a golfer. Some examples of it are jingling coins in your pocket while your opponent is putting or unjustly accusing him of a rules violation. It's not so much what happens that unsettles the opponent, but rather the idea that it did happen.

Whether or not an act is considered gamesmanship depends on the circumstances. If you're playing a five-dollar Nassau with the same three guys you've played with every weekend for thirteen years and you decide to burp in your opponent's backswing, that wouldn't be considered gamesmanship. (Actually, it would be considered quite funny in the author's group.) However, if you were playing in the Ryder Cup and suggested to your opponent that you think the ball he's playing is illegal when you know full well that's not the case, that would be gamesmanship. Over the course of his career, Seve Ballesteros was often accused of gamesmanship. When you're good at it, however, the accusations are the worst thing that can happen to you.

gap wedge A *gap wedge* is an iron with a loft somewhere between that of the pitching wedge and the sand wedge. Like the L wedge (see *L wedge*), the club isn't really necessary to play any specific shot, as the same results can be achieved by choking down on a pitching wedge. The *gap wedge* is an attempt by club manufacturers to convince Billy Joe Average that he has a "gap" in his game that needs filling.

gas When you leave a putt short, you might say, "It needed a little more gas." When you get tired of saying you choked or gagged, you can say you *took the gas*. It's nice for the sake of variety.

GC These two letters stand for golf club, and when you see them as part of a club name, you know the members mean business. (See *golf club*.)

gear effect If you want to impress your pals with your vast knowledge of engineering, tell them the *gear effect* between the club and the ball produced your hook. As they scratch their heads, tell them that the curved nature of the face of your old persimmon driver acting in concert with the angle at which you struck the ball, produced a gearlike effect, which resulted in the hook spin.

get down This is something you scream, normally after a brief sentence consisting almost entirely of obscenities, as your ball appears to be headed out-of-bounds, over the green, or anywhere else you don't want it to go. When you yell, "Oh, #$%*. Get down," what you mean is you want the ball to *get down* on the ground before it reaches the trouble.

get even A double-or-nothing bet, played for all the points compiled on a nine or a match. If you play *get evens*, you play them only on the ninth and eighteenth holes.

get lucky What you say to your ball when it's headed for trouble.

get one here When you and your partner are behind in a match and you feel as if you need to win the hole you're about to play to prevent the match from slipping away from you, look your partner in the eye and say, "We need to *get one here*." He'll know what you mean.

get shots If you're handicap is higher than someone you're playing with, you *get* the number of *shots* that is the difference between the two handicap numbers.

get up Though you yell at your ball to get down (see *get down*), you want to plead with it to *get up*. You have to be nicer to the ball if you want it to stay up in the air long enough to carry the water, clear the bunker, or reach the green. Sometimes it works.

Gilligan *Gilligan* is a variation on mulligan (see *mulligan*), a "free" second tee shot on the first hole of a round. Gilligan was the main character in the television sitcom *Gilligan's Island*.

gimme Being generous souls, we enjoy cutting our pals some slack when they hit the ball close to the hole, so we give putts (see *give a putt*) that we assume our opponents will make. Sportsmanship and all that good stuff. *Gimme* is a bastardization of the phrase *give me*. (We're good sports but lazy linguists.) So when you hit one to within about six inches of the hole and you want to know if Bobby Lockjaw is going to give it to you, you might say, "Is that a *gimme*?" If Bobby is feeling jaunty, you might not have to ask him because he may beat you to the punch by saying, "That's a gimme."

In stroke play, of course, you cannot give putts because players must hole out on each hole. However, *gimme* is still useful in stroke play. When you hit one close, your caddie might say to you, "That's in *gimme* range," meaning the ball is so close that it would be a gimme if it were possible under the rules.

Also, in both match play and stroke play, a putt that is close to the hole but isn't quite a certainty is often described as *no gimme*. This is frequently used when an approach putt goes beyond a comfortable distance from the hole, i.e., "That's no gimme coming back."

GIR An acronym for greens in regulation, the number or percentage of greens a player hits (stops his ball on in two shots less than par for the hole) in a given round, tournament, or tour season. The statistic is generally regarded as a measure of accuracy.

give a putt In match play, it is legal to concede a putt to your opponent. This means it's okay for you to indicate that you expect him to make his next putt. When you do so, it's okay for him to pick his ball up and tally his score as if he had indeed holed the putt. When

you concede the putt in such a manner, you are *giving the putt.* You would express it by saying either, "I'll give that to you," or "That's good," or "Take it (the ball) away."

give give If you and your opponent mutually decided to give each other putts (see *give a putt*), that's a *give give.*

give shots *Giving shots* is completely different from giving putts. If you're a four-handicap player and you're opponent is an eight-handicap, you will be giving him four shots during the round, one each on the four most difficult holes on the course. A commonly asked question before the start of a round is, "How many shots are you going to give me?" These first tee negotiations are among golf's most colorful moments.

goat farm A course that is in poor shape is sometimes referred to as a *goat farm.*

goer A goer is the same as a flier (see *flier*), in other words, a shot that flies a bit farther than typical for the club used.

go for it It's the final round of the Masters, and you're one shot off the lead. (Work with me here, please.)

You're standing in the fifteenth fairway, and you have to carry your next shot 225 yards to clear the pond in front of the green and give yourself a shot at eagle. You could play short of the pond and have an easier shot and a chance at birdie, but you're running out of holes. You decide to attempt the riskier shot and go for the greater reward. Later on, when you're wearing the green jacket (see *green jacket*) and talking to those stupid reporters, you'll tell them you talked it over with your caddie and decided to *go for it* at the fifteenth. Of course, if you decide to go for it and knock it in the water, you'll be the stupid one and the reporters will be the smart ones.

Gogliak When you hit a *Gogliak*, you've hit a dropkick (see *dropkick*), a shot with a wood where the club glances off the ground before it contacts the ball. *Gogliak* is a slang term derived from the name of the NFL's first soccer-style kicker, Pete Gogolak of the New York Giants.

going hook A *going hook* is one played with the intention of the ball running to its target once it hits the ground.

going low In a high-low match (see *high-low*), you're *going low* when you play for the low ball on your team.

Golden Bear Nickname for Jack Nicklaus, the greatest competitive golfer of all time. If you want to sound really cool, just call him *the Bear*.

STAN BADZ/PGA TOUR

Jack Nicklaus, "the Golden Bear," in 1996.

golfaholic If you're an alcoholic, you drink too much. If you're a workaholic, you work too much. You have one guess to determine what it is you do too much of if you're a *golfaholic*.

golf ball Be cool, just call it a ball. Only nerdy teaching pros and television announcers call it a *golf ball*, as if to distinguish it from the basketballs people sometimes use while playing golf.

golf club This term has two meanings. A *golf club* is the thing you swing in an effort to strike the ball. Winston Churchill called them "implements ill-suited for the task." (Needless to say, Mr. Churchill didn't do very well on his few attempts at the game.) You're better off just calling it a *club*.

A *golf club* is also a private club, the members of which play golf on the course at the club. When a private club is called a golf club as opposed to a country club, it's an important distinction. The words *golf club* after the proper name of the club indicate that its membership views golf as their primary pursuit. They don't have time for the silliness of tennis and swimming. They leave that to the members of country clubs. (See *country club*.)

golf course The *golf course* is the playing field for the game. A typical course consists of eighteen holes. Just call it a course—drop the *golf* or you'll sound like Jerry Pate.

The course at River Highlands.

SAM GREENWOOD/PGA TOUR

golf course design The practice of golf course architecture is sometimes referred to as *golf course design* or, more commonly, *course design*.

golfdom This is certainly the silliest word in the game. *Golfdom* refers to the entire world or universe of golf— all its players, courses, officials, organizations, destinations, tournaments, hangers-on, manufacturers, publications, television shows, and so forth. It's the whole shooting match. Frankly, the term makes golf sound as if it is a significant factor in the survival of mankind. Using the word will make you sound like an ass.

golfer This means you, Jack. Anyone who plays golf is a *golfer*. Whether or not you're a "real" golfer is another matter entirely.

golfiana Another fairly silly term, it refers to artifacts of the game, such as old clubs, old books and magazines, old medals. If you're into collecting such things, just say, "I collect stuff," and leave *golfiana* to the all of the nerds in golfdom.

golfing When you are out on the course playing golf, you are *golfing*. Sounds simple enough, but there are those who would argue that no real golfer would use this word or that it's not a word at all. The logic of the antigolfing movement goes something like this: Golf is the name of the sport; therefore you play golf, and while you're doing it, you are playing golf. (As an example of the lack of credibility this word carries, the Golfers Against Golfing (GAG?) cite such games as baseball. You've never heard of anyone "baseballing," have you? Or "tennising"? Who can say for sure what's gotten into the antigolfing golfer. Fact is, when you're playing golf, you're *golfing*. Too many people say it for it to be considered a non-word.

golf glove Many golfers prefer to wear a single *golf glove*, typically made of leather, for full shots. The glove improves the player's grip on the club—or at least it improves their perception of their grip. As if golf weren't goofy enough, right-handed players wear the glove on the left hand, and left-handed players do the opposite. Actually, there's a reason for this: The gloved hand has more direct contact with the club.

golf gods When things are going well for you on the course, the *golf gods* are smiling upon you. When your game is in the tank, the *golf gods* aren't pleased

with you. If you're a real golfer, you won't talk about the golf gods. You can save that for the people with no sense of humor.

Golf House Golf House is the headquarters of the United States Golf Association, and it's located in Far Hills, New Jersey. If you are passionate about museums and libraries and you're a golfer, you should visit Golf House.

golf lawyer A most despicable character, the *golf lawyer* mis-uses the Rules of Golf to gain an unethical advantage over those who don't know any better. If you catch one in the act, tarring and feathering is considered appropriate punishment for the perpetrator.

golf professional A *golf professional* is a person who makes a living servicing the general population of golfers. Sometimes referred to as a club pro, the typical *golf professional* is a jack-of-all-trades—part merchandiser, part teacher, part tournament administrator, part baby-sitter to his membership and customers. There is a rather significant distinction between a golf professional and a professional golfer. The latter specializes in tournament play and vanity, while the former specializes in down-to-earth, person-to-person values.

golf school A business enterprise that specializes in the mass production of golf lessons. Typically, the students at a *golf school* are taught in groups by an instructor.

golf shop The golf shop once was the golf professional's place of business, located on the grounds of the club or course that employed him. Today, a *golf shop* is any place of business that is devoted specifically to selling golf products regardless of whether it is located at a club or course or at the intersection of Elm Street and Oak Avenue and regardless of whether the proprietor is a golf professional or an ordinary businessman. (Also see *greengrass shop.*)

golf widow When a fellow's interest in the game exceeds his interest in his wife, she is a *golf widow.*

good, that's When you want to give your opponent a putt (see *give a putt*), you might say, "*That's good.*"

good good When two players devoid of self-confidence meet in a match, there are usually a few *good goods.* Here's how it works: Bobby Yips has a three-foot putt for par, and so does his opponent, Joey Shakes. Bobby is afraid he'll miss his putt and lose the hole. Funny enough, Joey is afraid he'll miss his putt and lose the hole. At this moment of mutual self-doubt, Joey and Bobby look at each other. "Good good?" says Bobby, meaning that both putts could be conceded and the hole halved. Joey says, "Yeah, good good," and the two spineless golfers have saved themselves the possible embarrassment and stress created by a missed short putts.

good miss Sometimes you hit a crummy shot and it turns out okay. Perhaps you hit a drive out on the toe of your driver, and the shot hooks back into the fairway. Or maybe you hit an iron thin, and it bounces up onto the green. That's what you call a *good miss*—an imperfect strike of the ball that produces a result better than you deserve.

gooseneck A type of iron, the *gooseneck,* features a slight bend or curve in the hosel that moves the lead edge (see *lead edge*) of the club farther back than standard.

gopher To be conversant regarding the movie *Caddyshack*, you need to know that a dancing *gopher* was the nemesis of Bill Murray's character, Carl the Greenkeeper.

gorse A gnarled shrub that features bright yellow flowers. There's only two things you need to know about *gorse*: You'll find it only on a true links course, and it subsists on a steady diet of golf balls.

got ahead of it This is one of the great excuses for a lousy shot because few people will know what you're talking about and no one will know if you're correct. Any time you push or slice one just say, "I *got ahead of it*," and everyone will nod in appreciation that you know your swing so well. The expression refers to the idea that your body *got ahead* in the swing and left the clubhead (*it*) behind. Since there are countless reasons for pushing and slicing, this excuse works well in covering them all.

got all of that one When you hit a shot well, particularly a tee shot, you might say, "I *got all of that one*."

got away with one If you strike what you feel is a poor shot but the result is not calamitous, you *got away with one*. If you and your partner play a sloppy hole but you end up tying or winning the hole anyway, you got away with one.

[I] got high. You take low. Some betting games are played for two points per hole (see *high-low*), and this is a nice way of telling your partner you're in the midst of butchering the current hole and your ball will be the high ball on your team. You'll know you have a supportive partner if he says, "No problem." If he hits you over the head with his seven-wood, you'll know he failed to see the humor of the comment.

go to school When you were a kid and you spent all day in school, the idea was that you would learn something—if you paid attention. When your ball is on the green and appears that it will take the same approximate line as the ball of someone who is farther away than you are, you are in a position to *go to school* on his putt. That is to say, you might just learn something about how your own putt will act on the green—if you pay attention.

grab There are more things to grab than you might think. Your ball can *grab* the green, which means it stopped quickly. More often than not, however, this is used in a negative sense, as in, "His ball didn't grab."

Also, in high grass, there is a tendency for the clubhead to get tangled in the grass and twist, causing an off-line shot. When this happens, the grass has *grabbed* the clubhead.

Finally, if you move into the lead of your match or a tournament, you have *grabbed* the lead.

grain This has nothing to do with a high fiber diet. The *grain* is the overall direction in which the grass is growing on a putting green. Some greens have no grain, others have lots of it, which makes them *grainy*. The importance of the grain is that a ball running into the grain (against the way the grass is leaning) will move slower, while a ball running with the grain (the same direction the grass is leaning) will go faster. Likewise, a putt breaking into the grain will break less, and a putt breaking with the grain will break more.

grand slam Golf's equivalent to the Holy Grail is the *grand slam*, which is the winning of all four of golf's major championships in the same year. No one has won the modern grand slam, which consists of the Masters, the U.S. Open, the British Open, and the U.S.

PGA Championship (see *major championships*). The closest anyone has come was in 1953 when Ben Hogan won the Masters and both Opens. He didn't play in the PGA Championship due to a schedule conflict. No one has won more than two majors in a given year since then. So difficult is it to complete a grand slam that only four players (Gene Sarazen, Hogan, Jack Nicklaus, and Gary Player) have won each of the majors at least once during their entire careers.

The legendary amateur player Bobby Jones captured the game's only grand slam in 1930 when the four major championships were the U.S. Open and Amateur and the British Open and Amateur. Even then the task was daunting, with some calling the four events the "impregnable quadrilateral."

grandstand The *grandstand* is where galleryites (see *gallery*) park their carcasses when they don't feel like walking. It is also the tournament player's friend because a really lousy shot often ends up in or against the grandstand, which stops the progress of the ball and entitles the player to a free drop.

graphite *Graphite* is the all-encompassing term for various hybrids of elements used to make club parts such as shafts and clubheads. Graphite's inclusion in the equipment mainstream coincided with that of the metal wood. Graphite's appeal is that it is lighter than steel and thus can increase the speed at which the club moves.

grass bunker A bunker (see *bunker*) that has only grass in it.

Great Triumvirate Never in the history of golf has there been a such dominant force as the *Great Triumvirate* of Harry Vardon, J. H. Taylor, and James Braid. From 1894 to 1914, these three

CORBIS-BETTMANN

J.H. Taylor, James Braid, and Harry Vardon

giants accounted for sixteen British Open championships—six by Vardon and five apiece by Taylor and Braid.

green The closely mown putting surface where the hole is cut. Also, in the old days, the Scots called the entire course the *green*.

green, through the A phrase that relates only to the Rules of Golf, *through the green* means the entire golf course except the tee and the green on the hole you're playing and all hazards on the course.

green committee At a private club, the *green committee* is a group of members who make decisions regarding course maintenance and course setup.

green fee The *green fee* is the money you pay to play at a golf course.

greengrass shop A highfalutin way of saying pro shop, *greengrass* refers to on-course golf shops run by golf professionals. The term became popular with the advent of off-course discount golf shops, as it differentiates between the two types of golf shops.

green high When your ball misses the green but lands to either side of it and parallel with it, you're ball is *green high*. The expression provides solace after a stinker of a shot.

greenie A greenie is a side bet within a larger betting match. To win a *greenie*, which is up for grabs only on par three holes, you must do two things: hit the green and be closest to the hole. If you're on the green and you're 80 feet from the hole and everyone else has missed the green, you win the greenie—even if Uncle Bob is on the fringe, eight feet from the hole. That's why the bet is called a *greenie* and not a *fringie*.

green in regulation When your ball comes to rest on a green in two shots less than the par for that hole, you have hit the *green in regulation*. (And if you hit a par five in two shots or drive the green on a par four, that counts, too.) *Regulation* in this sense means normal or regular, and it indicates the number of shots an excellent player would normally take to reach a given green.

green jacket If you've won the Masters or you're a member of the Augusta National Golf Club, you have a *green jacket* emblazoned with the club's logo on the breast pocket. It's an ugly jacket, but any golfer who

doesn't have one would do just about anything to get one. There's one catch, however: You can't wear the jacket to your local bar to impress your pals. Only the reigning Masters champion is permitted to remove his jacket from the club grounds.

greenkeeper The employee of a club or golf course who is responsible for the maintenance of the course. Nowadays the *greenkeeper* is often referred to as the green superintendent. The greenkeeper's profession is known as *greenkeeping*. An interesting note on this term: There is no s in *greenkeeper*—the first part of the word uses the old Scottish word *green*, meaning the entire golf course.

greenside Just about anything located near a green is considered *greenside*, but the typical use for this word is to describe the location of a bunker, i.e., a *greenside bunker*.

grillroom The *grillroom* is the place you drink beer (and maybe even eat something) after your round and bore everyone with tales of how well you played. Grillrooms are often segregated according to gender and in such cases are denoted as men's grill and women's or ladies' grill.

grinder A golfer who never loses the intensity of his concentration or resolve, regardless of circumstances, is a *grinder*. When these traits are obvious to any onlooker, the player is said to be *grinding*.

grip The end of the club you hold while swinging is referred to as the *grip* end of the club. The rubber or leather cover on that end of the club is called a *grip*, as is the manner and action of placing your hands on the club.

grip it and rip it This phrase became popular with the emergence of professional golf's original "Wild Thing," John Daly, one of the longest hitters in the history of the game. After winning the 1991 PGA Championship, Daly's freewheeling, long-hitting style became known simply as *grip it and rip it*, a reference to the fact that he simply held the club and tried to hit the ball as far as possible.

grip pressure The amount of pressure you apply with your hands to the club is known as *grip pressure*.

grocery The monies being contested for in a betting match are sometimes referred to as *the grocery*, the allusion being that some golfers are stupid enough to gamble with their grocery money.

groove Each line on the face of your club is a *groove*, and together they are called the grooves. The grooves help get the ball airborne and create spin on the ball.

Also, when everything is clicking and your swing feels automatic, you're in a *groove*. When you've perfected your swing or a certain shot as the result of persistent practice, you've *grooved* that element of your swing.

gross Your *gross score* for a hole or a round is the score you make before deducting (or adding) handicap strokes.

grounder A shot that never gets in the air, but was struck with the intention of it doing so, is a *grounder*.

ground the club When the club touches the ground as you're addressing your ball, it has been *grounded*. It is illegal to ground your club in a hazard, and if you ground your club at address and the ball subsequently moves, that's a penalty, too. That's why players such as Jack Nicklaus and Greg Norman never *ground the club*.

ground under repair *Ground under repair* is any place on the course that is undergoing maintenance work or has been determined to need maintenance. Ground under repair is indicated by an outline of white paint on the ground. If your ball is within such a circle, you are entitled to relief.

group lesson When you take lessons from a professional at the same time as several other people, you're part of a *group lesson*. This typically occurs at a golf school.

growl A shot that has some *growl* on it is a shot that shows some teeth, i.e., it bites the green (see *bite*).

grow teeth This is a much funnier way of asking your ball to stop or bite (see *bite*). When you say *grow teeth*, do so loudly and with a big grin on your face.

gunch Slang for rough (see *rough*).

gutta-percha Golf's original ball, the featherie (see *featherie*) was prone to damage when struck with the edge of an iron club. The more durable gutta-percha ball replaced the featherie around 1848. The *gutta-percha* was made from the sap of trees found in Malaysia and was frequently referred to as a *gutty*.

H

hack When on a given day your game is bad from top to bottom—just plain lousy in every aspect—your poor play could be described as *hacking*, and afterwards you can say in disgust, "Ah, I hacked." Just a bad day though, right? However, if you play like a dog every time out, you are a full-blooded *hack* or *hacker*.

Also, when a ball is in extremely deep rough and you have no chance to make clean contact with it, you take a *hack* at it and try to advance it forward.

Hagen, Walter One of the great characters in the history of the game,

Walter Hagen in 1928.

CORBIS-BETTMANN

Hagen is best know for his light-hearted attitude and savvy match play instincts. He is credited with originating a favorite saying of golfers, namely, "Never hurry, never worry, and always take time to smell the flowers." His breezy personality belied his competitive nature, however. He won five PGA Championships at match play, including four in a row from 1924 through 1927. He also won four British Opens and two U.S. Opens, including the 1914 Open, the year after Francis Ouimet's stunning victory in that event (see *Ouimet, Francis*).

half a point In team match play competition, when a match is tied after eighteen holes, each of the teams receives *half a point* toward its total score.

half shot A *half shot* is any shot played with a swing that is approximately half as long as would be used for a full shot with the selected club. Half shots are normally played with wedges, the shorter swing allowing the player to hit the ball shorter distances.

halfway house When you're standing in the middle of the ninth fairway and your thoughts turn to hot dogs and beer, help is only a few hundred yards away. God invented the *halfway house*,

typically a small building serving a light food menu and drinks to go, so weary golfers could refresh themselves before tackling the back nine. The *halfway house* is usually located between the ninth green and the tenth tee.

halve In match play when a hole ends in a tie, it is said to be *halved*, with neither player or side gaining points. If the overall match ends in a tie, it too is *halved*.

ham-and-egg When you and your partner have a propensity for alternating spurts of good play, you are a *ham-and-egg* partnership. You know you're ham-and-egging when you play a hole well and your partner tanks it, and he plays well while you're hacking on a hole.

ham-and-ham When you and your partner both play well at the same moments and poorly at the same moments, you're *ham-and-hamming* it.

handicap A *handicap* is a compensation that allows players of all abilities to compete under equal circumstances. Your *handicap* is basically established by determining your average score over a number of rounds, always taking into account your most recent rounds. When a player with a high handicap (a player who averages high scores) plays a player with a low handicap, the high-handicapper gets to deduct shots from his score on certain holes on the course, the holes being rated in order of difficulty. The number of shots deducted is determined by the difference between the two handicaps. In matches involving four players, each of the three high-handicappers get to deduct the number of shots equivalent to the difference between their own handicap and that of the low-handicapper.

handle To avoid the confusion that arises from the multiple uses for the word *grip*, the end of the club that the player holds while swinging is sometimes referred to as the *handle*.

hand mashie A euphemism for the act of throwing the ball out of a bunker with your hand. The *hand mashie* is typically used in moments of tremendous disgust with oneself and, of course, is an admission that you are giving up for the hole.

hands player Players, like Chi Chi Rodriguez, who have active hands and wrists during their swing, particularly in the takeaway (see *takeaway*) and through impact, are commonly called *hands players*, with their swings being

SAM GREENWOOD/PGA TOUR

Chi Chi Rodriguez's swing is considered "handsy."

classified as *handsy*. The term is not derogatory in any sense.

hanging lie When the ball sits above your feet, i.e, you're on unlevel terrain and the ball is higher than your feet, you have a *hanging lie*. Aim right because you're going to hook it, then tell your pals you had a *hanger*.

hang one out there When you *hang one out there*, it means you aimed your shot with the intention of it drawing (curving gently from right to left), only to see it start out to the right and stay to the right (*hang out there*).

happy feet When you have *happy feet*, it's not a good thing. This term refers to the fact that you're nervous and appear to have trouble settling into shots or prematurely finish the swing or stroke or both.

hardpan When your ball is sitting on ground so hard you couldn't take a divot with a jackhammer, you're on *hardpan*. Shots from hardpan require a precision swing because the club will bounce off the ground if it hits behind the ball.

Hawk One of a few nicknames for Ben Hogan, one of the game's all-time best players.

hazard A *hazard* is a feature of a golf course designed to penalize errant shots. Bunkers with sand in them and water are the two basic *hazards* in golf. Sometimes a deep ravine or ditch is also marked as a hazard. There is no relief from hazards, and you cannot ground your club or move loose impediments while preparing to play from one. If there's a bright side to hazards, it's that there is no penalty for playing the wrong ball in one.

hazard line The perimeter of a water hazard is marked by stakes driven into the ground. The imaginary line between these stakes is the *hazard line*, and once you or your ball crosses it, you're in the hazard. In professional tournament play, the hazard line is clearly defined by spraying paint on the ground around the perimeter of the hazard.

head The *head* of the club is the part designed to contact the ball. It is short for clubhead.

headcover Intended to protect the heads of woods from being scuffed, *headcovers* slip easily over the clubheads and are typically made of a knit material or leather. Some exotic headcovers are made of fur, and there are plastic versions for irons. No real golfer would be caught dead with iron covers.

heel The *heel* of the clubface is the part that joins with the hosel (see *hosel*).

Hell Bunker A massive bunker on the fourteenth hole at the Old Course (see *Old Course*), *Hell Bunker* is a pit of death from which few golfers escape unscathed.

Hell's Half-Acre A gigantic bunker that dissects the fairway of the seventh hole at Pine Valley Golf Club (see *Pine Valley Golf Club*), *Hell's Half-Acre* must be carried on the second shot on the par-five hole.

hickory shaft From the late 1800s through the 1920s, the shafts of golf clubs were made of hickory wood.

high-low This refers to a match wherein two partners pit their high ball on a given hole and their low ball on a given hole against the high and low balls of their opponents.

Two points are available on each hole. For example, if you and Lenny are partners and you make a four on the hole and Lenny makes five, your ball is the low ball and Lenny's is the high ball. Your ball would be matched against the low ball of your opponents. If your opponents' low ball was a five, you would win a point. If your opponents' high ball was also a five (that is, they both made five), Lenny's ball would tie their high ball, and your team would win a total of one point for the hole.

high side The point on the circumference of a hole that faces the direction from which an approaching putt will break is the *high side* of the hole.

Himalayas, the The 201-yard fifth hole at Prestwick Golf Club in Scotland is known as *the Himalayas* because the tee ball must clear a gigantic dune that blocks a view of the green.

hit When you play a stroke, you have *hit* a shot. When your tee shot lands in the fairway, you have *hit* that fairway. When your ball lands on the green of the hole you're playing in two shots less than the par for the hole, you have *hit* the green in regulation.

hit and hold This expression refers to the act of striking the ball (the hit) and then preventing the clubhead from turning closed in the follow-through by holding on tighter with the left hand and guarding against the left wrist breaking. The image of the *hit and hold* is most commonly used to describe how to play a knockdown shot (see *knockdown shot*).

hit and hope Sometimes when your ball is amidst trees and you have no clear avenue to get it back into play, your only choice is to play a *hit and hope*. That is to say, you pick a spot, hit the ball, and hope it doesn't hit any trees or branches and makes it safely to its destination.

hit from the heels When you swing as hard as you possibly can, you're *hitting from the heels*, an expression based on the fact that when you swing very fast, you're apt to lose your balance and end up with your weight on the heels of your feet—precisely where it shouldn't be.

hit it so hard it started to bleed What you might say after you really pound a drive.

hitter There are two types of golfers, swingers and hitters. A *hitter* makes every move in his swing action based on hitting the ball. A swinger concentrates on swinging the club and lets the ball get in the way of the club. John Daly is a hitter while a player such as Payne Stewart would be considered a swinger.

hockey a putt When you hit a lousy putt or several lousy putts on a given hole, you'd say you *hockeyed the putt*, which refers to the fact that you hit it as if you were swinging a hockey stick.

Hogan, Ben One of the finest competitive players in history, Ben Hogan was noted for his precision play and fierce desire to win. He won four U.S. Opens, two PGA Championships, two Masters titles, and one British Open,

Ben Hogan in 1953.

the latter in his only appearance in the event (1953). In 1953, Hogan came as near as anyone ever has to winning golf's grand slam (see *grand slam*) when he won the Masters and both Opens. A scheduling conflict prevented him from playing in the PGA Championship. He is also well-known for his dramatic comeback from a near fatal accident in 1949 when the car he was driving was crushed by a bus. Actually, the prime of his career came after the accident. In later years when asked if he had any advice for young players, Hogan responded, "Watch out for buses."

Hogan's Alley Nickname for Riviera Country Club in Pacific Palisades, California, where Ben Hogan won two Los Angeles Opens and one U.S. Open in the space of two years (1947 and 1948). Some also refer to Colonial

Country Club in Forth Worth, Texas, as Hogan's Alley, since Hogan was from the area and played well at Colonial.

hog back A *hog back* is a fairway or a green with a clearly defined ridge.

hold A shot *holds* when it lands on the green and bounces little or not at all. When a particular green or all of the greens on a course are prone to receive shots in such a manner, you would say they are *holding*.

Also, when you are leading a tournament or match, you are *holding* the lead.

hole The *hole* in the ground into which you try to hit your ball is 4¼ inches in diameter. In a larger sense, the term *hole* also applies to each of the eighteen elements of a golf course that start at a tee and end at a green. When your ball goes into the hole in the ground, you are said to have *holed* it. In match play, the score is kept by adding up the number of holes a player wins. When there appears to be a realistic opportunity for a putt or a chip to be holed, you might say something such as, "This one looks *holeable*."

hole high When your ball is level with the hole, regardless of whether or not the ball is on the green, you (and your ball) are *hole high*.

hole in one A ball played into the hole in a single stroke.

hole liner The device placed inside the hole, once it is cut, to hold the flagstick and to prevent the hole from collapsing.

hole out When you play a shot into the hole, you have *holed out*.

hole sign A *hole sign*, placed near the tee box (see *tee box*) on a given hole, usually displays information pertaining to the par and yardages from the various tees.

Hollywood When things are going good, when shot after shot feels good, looks good, and is good, you're *Hollywood*, baby.

home Home may be where the heart is, but it's also where you want your ball to go. If you are attempting to reach the green from a substantial distance away—let's say you're trying to reach the green of a par five with your second shot—you are trying to *get home*. So you might ask your caddie, "Do you think I can get home from here?" If he nods with approval, he thinks you can reach the green with the shot you're about to play.

The final or back nine holes of a golf course are sometimes known as the *home nine*. Also, when the holes remaining in a round play in general toward the clubhouse, the course is said to *turn home* or *turn for home*, *home* in this sense meaning the clubhouse. Likewise, when the players reach these holes, they are said to be *heading for home* or *turning for home*.

home-and-home In matches between two golf clubs, a set of matches is referred to as *home-and-home* when each club serves once as the venue for play.

home hole The final hole on a golf course.

honor On the first tee of a match, the first player to hit off is determined by drawing lots, flipping a coin, or some similar method of chance. After, the player or team with the low score on the previous hole plays off first and is said to have the *honor* or *honors*.

hood A term that describes the tilting forward of the clubhead, which reduces the effective loft (see *effective loft*) of the club. To *hood* the club, you can do one of two things: move your hands farther ahead of the ball or move the ball farther back in your stance.

You might choose to hood the club if you wish to pick up a few extra yards with a given club or if you wanted to hit the ball on a lower trajectory than is typical for the selected club.

hook A shot that, in general, curves out of control from right to left. The flight of the ball is described as a *hook*, as is the act of hitting it. There is such a thing as a controlled hook—a severely bending shot played to go around an obstacle such as a tree. If you hit a lot of hooks, you're a *hooker*.

horses for courses The *horses for courses* theory holds that certain players perform very well on certain golf courses. You would typically hear this in reference to a player on a professional tour who has been consistently successful on a given course.

hosel The part of the clubhead, particularly on irons, that acts as a receptacle for the shaft. The *hosel* is the part of the club that contacts the ball to create a shank (see *shank*). Some players refer to a shank as a hosel shot or a hosel job.

hot When you're playing so good it's almost surreal, you're *hot*.

How'd that stay out? An expression of dismay frequently used after a ball narrowly misses going in the hole.

Also, used as a humorous, sarcastic expression when a putt ends up nowhere near the hole.

hump An expression used by caddies to describe the walking part of their job. When a caddie is out on the course moving around, he's *humping*.

hunched A player with poor posture at address, who slouches his shoulders down to hold the club rather than tipping forward from the waist, is said to be *hunched*. Also, the putting stance of certain players who crouch low to the ground is said to be *hunched*. Jack Nicklaus and Arnold Palmer, as young men at least, hunched over the ball.

hustler A golfer who likes to bet and typically picks opponents based on the fact that he knows he can beat them.

I

iffy After you hit an errant shot and the outcome of it is not clear to you, you would describe the situation to your partner as *iffy*, i.e., it could be okay or it could be in trouble.

I got that shot When a situation calls for a specific shot and you feel as if you can effectively execute that shot, you might say, with all the confidence in the world, "*I got that shot.*" You won't impress your pals with your grammar, but they'll think you know you're good—at least until you hit the shot.

Ike's Pond The pond that wraps around the front and left of the sixteenth green at Augusta National Golf Club. *Ike's Pond* is named for President Dwight Eisenhower (Ike was his nickname), who was a member at the club.

Ike's Tree Once President Eisenhower was through hitting balls into the pond that bears his name at Augusta National Golf Club, he'd walk over to the seventeenth tee and watch his tee shot whack a lone tree that stands in the left side of that fairway. He hit it so much, they named it after him.

impact When the clubhead collides with the ball at the bottom of the swing, that's *impact*. In swing talk, it's described as the *impact position*.

President Eisenhower became the namesake for several features at Augusta National Golf Club.

impact zone This refers to the part of your swing beginning just prior to impact and ending just after impact.

improved lie Sometimes, due to less than ideal course conditions or the fact that they don't care to play by the rules, players agree to improve their lies by moving their balls from the positions at which they come to rest to nearby ground they deem satisfactory for playing the shots. This is against the games most basic rule of playing

the ball as it lies. But what the hell, if everyone in your group agrees to do it, no one is harmed.

improve your lie Golf's single most important rule is to play the ball as it lies. Mess with your lie so you can hit a better shot and you're *improving your lie.*

in As you play the last nine holes of a course, you are playing *in*, or in toward the clubhouse.

individual Most betting matches are of a team nature, with two players competing as partners against two other players. For the hardy gambler, this often does not provide enough action, so he plays individual matches against one or more players in the group. These bets are in addition to the team bets and are simply referred to as *individuals.*

inland course Any golf course that is not situated along a coastline or a large body of water is known as an *inland course.*

insert Wooden drivers had plastic *inserts* in the center of the face to prevent the club from eroding due to constant impact. Jack Nicklaus, as a very young man, hit the ball so hard that he cracked four inserts in a single year.

108

Most golfers never cracked the inserts on their clubs.

inside-out swing This is a term to describe one of the two general swing paths (see *swing path*) your club can take during the swing. To understand the image of an *inside-out swing*, imagine a straight line extending from the back of the ball. During an inside-out swing, the clubhead moves into the ball from inside that line (in other words, closer to you). After impact, the club never actually crosses that line, but the feeling during the swing is that the clubhead crosses that line or moves to the outside of that line.

inside the leather Some golfers like to use the standard of inside the leather for determining whether or not a putt is good (see *good, that's*). The leather is the grip on a putter. Any putt shorter than the distance of the exposed shaft on a putter (*inside the leather*) is good in such circumstances. To measure, a golfer would place the clubhead inside the hole and lay the putter on the ground.

interlocking grip One of the two basic methods for gripping the club is the *interlocking grip*, the distinguishing feature of which is the left pinky finger interlocking with the right index finger. Most top level players do not use the interlocking grip; however, Jack Nicklaus is one very notable exception.

intermediate target Many golfers have learned it's easier to aim at something close to you as opposed to something far away (like your target). What they do is pick out something on the ground close to them—a twig, a leaf, or a patch of grass—that also happens to be on the same line (see *line*) as the eventual target. The player then aims the clubhead at the thing he picked out, his *intermediate target*.

in my pocket When, on a given hole, you grow disgusted with your play and decide to pick up (see *pick up*), you might declare to the group, "I'm *in my pocket*," which is where you place your ball after you take it out of play.

in the hunt Any player is *in the hunt* when he has a reasonable chance of winning a tournament heading into or during the final round or when he is near the leader at the completion of any given round

in the linen If *in my pocket* sounds a bit too common for you, you can opt for *in the linen* as a substitute. You don't have to be wearing linen pants to do so.

in the money In professional tournament play when a player makes the cut (see *cut*), he is guaranteed to pick up at least a little cash as a prize and therefore is said to finish *in the money*.

iron This general term describes the bladelike clubs generally made from steel (not including metal woods) that make up the bulk of a player's set of clubs. The typical set of irons is manufactured to produce predictable and consistent yardage variations in the shots played with them. Some modern iron clubheads are made of graphite but are still referred to as irons because the word has come to mean the type of club as opposed to the material from which it is made.

Iron Byron A mechanical ball-striking machine used to test golf clubs and golf balls, so named because its swing path is based on that of Byron Nelson.

island green Any green that is completely surrounded by water is an *island green*. The most famous (or infamous) of this species is the seventeenth hole at the TPC at Sawgrass (see *TPC* and *TPC at Sawgrass*), in Ponte Vedra, Florida, home of the Players Championship.

Is that any good? A terribly annoying, rhetorical question posed by jerks after they hit a good shot.

It ain't a beauty contest What you should say after you win or tie a hole despite some less than perfect shots, particularly if your opponent starts whining because he can't believe his two perfect shots didn't win it for him.

It's in the hole What Bill Murray's *Caddyshack* character, Carl, said as he butchered the flowers at Bushwood Country Club with a sickle. At the time, Carl was playing his imaginary approach shot to the final green at Augusta National.

The Iron Byron mimics the swing of golf legend Byron Nelson, here in 1945.

AP/WIDE WORLD PHOTOS

J

Jack and Jill A type of club tournament where a man and woman form a team and compete against other teams with the same makeup.

jail When you hit a really, really bad shot that leaves you in a heap of trouble, you might say, "*That's jail,*" to indicate that you have very little chance of escaping from the predicament.

jelly legs A player who is nervous or tired has *jelly legs*, which means he's feeling weak or a bit wobbly.

jerk When you pull a putt left of the hole, you might say you *jerked* it. Also, it's not a bad word to describe the way you played after a poor round.

jigger When clubs had names, a *jigger* was a club designed for playing lofted pitch shots.

Jones, Bobby The greatest of all amateur golfers and damned near better than every pro that ever played, Bobby Jones is best remembered for three things. First, he won the grand slam (see *grand slam*) in 1930, the only golfer to win any variation of golf's Holy Grail. Second, he founded the Augusta National Golf Club (see *Augusta National Golf Club*) and the Masters Tournament (see *Masters*). Finally, Jones is remembered as embodying golf as a gentleman's game. All told, Jones won 13 major championships (four U.S. Opens, five U.S.

Bobby Jones in 1930.

AP/WIDE WORLD PHOTOS

Amateurs, three British Opens, one British Amateur), which is still second all-time to Jack Nicklaus.

juice *Juice* is spin on the ball. When you hit a shot that hits the green and spins, you might say it had juice on it. Also, when you really smash a drive, you might say it was juiced.

juicy lie When your ball is sitting up on a nice, fluffy pile of rough and you can get a clean hit on it, you have a *juicy lie*. The term refers to the fact that the grass that produces this lie is rich and thick, having soaked up lots of water so that the blades appear more plump or *juicy* than normal.

jump Every so often, the ball will come off the face of the club with a bit more force than you anticipated. A good excuse in this situation is to say, "Oh, it *jumped* on me."

Also, when you have a flier lie (see *flier*), you might say you expect the ball to *jump* or fly farther than it normally would with the club you've selected.

jump on it When you need to hit the ball a few more yards than you would normally attempt with a certain club, you would say you're going to *jump on it*. This situation usually occurs when you are between clubs (see *between clubs*) and decide that you're better off trying to stretch the distance of the shorter club rather than attempting to hit an eased up version of the longer club.

jungle Tangled, thick, long rough is sometimes referred to as *jungle*. Also, some of your pals might ask you about your trip to the *jungle* as you emerge from the trees.

junk When a betting match has several smaller bets in addition to the main bet—greenies (see *greenie*), polys (see *poly*), etc.—the smaller bets are known collectively as *junk*.

K

Kato, a When your opponent's shot gets a lucky bounce, and you see it but you can't believe it, that's a *Kato*, so named for Kato Kaelin, the infamous nonwitness in the O. J. Simpson murder trial.

keeper After you hit a very good shot and you want to sound cool, you just say, "That's a *keeper*." In other words, you don't feel the need to play the shot over again—you'll keep it.

kick When a ball in the air hits the ground, the resulting bounce is called a *kick*. When your shot is off target and you want it to bounce back toward the target, you'd say (while the ball is still in the air), "Get a good kick." When a ball headed toward the target veers offline due to the bounce, you got a bad kick. And when your ball looks as if it's going to come up short of the green and you think pleading with it may help to create a longer bounce that might get you home (see *home*), you would say, "Take a big kick."

kicker At some golf clubs, players put money into a *kicker* pool. A random number is chosen. Anyone who shoots a score that matches the number wins the kicker bet.

kick-in When you hit the ball so close to the hole that you could walk up and tap it in with your foot, that's called a *kick-in*.

kickpoint The point of maximum bend in a shaft is known as the *kickpoint*.

kicks and throws A betting game wherein each player is allowed two free kicks of the ball and two free throws of the ball on each nine. You can use these *kicks and throws* any time you choose.

kill In 1991, long-hitting John Daly captured the attention of golf fans everywhere when he won the PGA Championship. The story goes that his caddie simply muttered the word *kill* to Daly before each tee shot.

killed it When you hit a ball so hard you can almost hear it scream, you *killed* it.

kiltie From time to time, as fashions change, golf shoes are outfitted with flaps that cover the laces. The flaps are called *kilties*.

King, the Arnold Palmer's primary nickname. If you want to sound like you know golf, you simply call Arnold *the King*.

knee-knocker A *knee-knocker* is a putt of sufficient length to be challenging and that, particularly under pressure, might create a brain cramp in the player about to hit it. The expression refers to the idea that a nervous person might tremble and knock his knees together.

knife The one-iron. If you're good enough to hit one, you're cool enough to call it a *knife*.

knockdown shot A superb control shot struck with the irons, the *knockdown shot* is desirable for its predictable fade, low trajectory, and loads of spin. Players feel as if they can control this shot because the swing is compact and creates a feeling of control. The basics of playing the *knockdown* are the following: one more club than typical for the distance, a slightly open stance, the ball back in your stance, a three-quarter backswing, a hit-and-hold (see *hit and hold*) follow-through, allowance for a slight fade.

knocked it in After you hole out, you can say, "I *knocked it in*." Typically, this expression includes the club involved or the length of putt made, i.e., "I knocked it in with a wedge from off the green," or "I knocked in a 40-foot putt for birdie."

knockoff A club which is a copy or forgery of an original design is a *knock-off* club (see *clone*).

knowing where to miss it A good player always identifies (whenever possible) the spots where it will be okay for his ball to go in the event that it is not perfectly struck. This is called *knowing where to miss it.*

knuckleball A shot hit deep in the heel (see *heel*) is sometimes referred to as a *knuckleball* because of its odd feel and ball flight characteristics.

L

lag In the downswing, the angle between your hands and the clubhead (which doesn't catch up to your hands until impact) is known as *lag*.

lag putt On long putts, attempting to get the ball near the hole often makes more sense than trying to actually hole it. Such a putt is known as a *lag putt*. Often, such a putt would simply be described as a *lag*. Why not try to hole the putt? The odds are against you doing so, so you're better off ensuring that you have a makeable putt remaining.

laid back In an effort to hit a particular club slightly higher and shorter than normal, you might lay the clubface back. That is to say, you might lean the shaft away from the target to add to the effective loft (see *effective loft*) off the club.

laid off When you reach the top of your swing and the clubface is pointed directly at the sky, the club would be described as *laid off*. It's not a textbook position by any means.

large Hit a long shot and you've hit a *large* one. When your pal crushes one, just whistle and say, "That's *large*."

Larry Lag When you hit a lag putt, your partner might jokingly refer to you as *Larry Lag*.

lateral The dirtiest word in golf is *shank*. Players make up all sorts of terms to describe a such a shot, which flies on a line perpendicular to that intended. One such euphemism is *lateral*, a reference to the sideways toss in football and rugby.

lateral hazard A *lateral hazard* is typically a water hazard that, in general, runs parallel to the line of play as opposed to crossing the line of play.

launch angle The angle at which the ball leaves the clubface at impact.

launched When you hit a big tee shot, you can say you *launched* it. The air can get thin up there, partner, so be careful.

lay back When you decide to play a shot short of a hazard as opposed to attempting to carry it, you might say you've decided to *lay back*.

lay it dead To *lay it dead* means to hit the ball very close to the hole. It does not mean quite the same thing as simply saying your ball is dead (see *dead*).

layout A golf course is sometimes referred to as a *layout* because the course was laid out by an architect before it was built.

lay the sod over it When you hit and take a big old divot that curls up and covers the spot where your ball was only seconds before, you've *laid the sod over it*. You'll know you've done it when your buddies start laughing at you—again.

lay up Discretion is the better part of valor (or something like that), so when you're staring down the fairway at a pond or a huge bunker that looks like it is determined to eat your ball if you attempt to carry it, you might decide to *lay up*, or intentionally play a shot that will come up short of the hazard in question. The shot is called a *lay-up shot*.

lazy swing A *lazy swing* is one made with the arms only, without getting the rest of the body involved. Make a lot of these and you'll make a lot of high scores.

lead edge The *lead edge* of the club is the point where the bottom of the clubface meets the sole of the club.

118

More important, the *lead edge* is the part of the club you aim at the target.

leaderboard In professional tournament golf, large boards are placed around the course to show the scores of the players as they progress around the course. *Leaderboards* were first introduced at the Masters, with red numbers indicating under par scores and black numbers over par. Today, some leaderboards are electronic.

Also, when a player gets within a few shots of the lead in tournament play, he is said to be *on the leaderboard*.

leader in the clubhouse In stroke play tournaments, the player with the lowest posted score (see *posted score*) is considered the *leader in the clubhouse*, even though players still on the course may be on pace to shoot much lower scores.

leaf rule Not an actual Rule of Golf, the leaf rule is a way of speeding up play and lessening the frustration of playing golf in the fall—at least in regions with leafy trees. The *leaf rule* allows you to drop a ball without penalty if you believe you can't find your ball because it is under a leaf or leaves. Don't try this in competition,

but among friends it makes the game a bit more enjoyable.

leaking oil You started out the round playing great, and everything was going your way. Then you made a bogey here and a bogey there—no big blowup, mind you, just a steady stream of strokes piling up on your scorecard. Well, that slow, steady progression toward a bad score is known as *leaking oil*. When you're leaking oil, you don't have any single hole that kills you; it's simply overall poor play.

leaner From the term in horseshoes, when you hit a *leaner*, your ball is very, very close to the hole.

let him in When your partner hits a good putt that appears as if it may go in, you might say loud enough for all to hear, "Let him in."

let it fly When you swing free and easy, unencumbered by a brainful of swing mush, you're *letting it fly*. Chances are excellent the ball will do the same.

level When you're even in your match and the little Anglophile inside you wants to say something clever, try,

"I believe our match is *level*. Is that correct, Lester?" Also, when your score matches par at the end of or during your round, you are *level* par.

lie A common question in golf is, "What do you lie?" The person asking that question wishes to know how many strokes you've taken thus far on the hole you're playing. Your answer should be, "I *lie*—." (Fill in the blank with the number of strokes you've played to that point.)

Also, the angle at which the club-head is set in relation to the shaft of the club is known as the *lie* of the club. And the position of a resting ball is its *lie*.

lift, clean, and place In tournament play when the ground is exceedingly soft and muddy and the ball plugs (see *plug*) upon hitting the ground, players are sometimes allowed, under the Rules of Golf, to *lift, clean, and place*. This means they can pick up the ball (the lift), wipe it clean, and place it in the general vicinity of the original spot.

line The *line* is the route that a given shot should take. When you ask someone for a *line* on a full shot, he will generally indicate a point where you would like the shot to end up.

On the putting green the line is usually established as the point where the ball should be started, not where it will end up as a result of the green's contours. In other words, if you asked your caddie or partner for a line on a putt, the response might be "Start it about two inches right of the hole" or "It will slide left at the hole." What they are giving you is an indication of where you should aim the putt to start. (If you ask them for a line and they say, "So, you come here often?" you are within your rights to hit them in the shins with your putter.)

line of play The *line of play* is the path you expect the ball to take after you've hit it plus a reasonable distance on either side of that line. The line of play extends up into the air without limit but does not extend past the hole.

line of putt The *line of putt* is the line on the green you expect your ball to take after you stroke it. The *line of putt* extends from the hole and through your ball all the way to the end of the continent you happen to be playing on. This term is an important one to know because it is illegal for you or your caddie to touch the line of putt to indicate anything. A famous incident involving this term occurred during the third round of the 1991 PGA Championship when it appeared to some loser watching television that John Daly's caddie had touched the line of putt with the flagstick. After a brief debate, it was determined that the caddie, Jeff "Squeaky" Medlin, had not, in fact, touched the line of putt.

line up When you are in the act of determining the line for a putt or a full shot, you *line up* the shot.

links The term *links* is commonly used to refer to any golf course, but to sound like a real golfer, you should say *links* only when referring to a seaside course, specifically the seaside courses of England, Scotland, and Ireland. The term is derived from *linksland*, which describes ground uncovered when the sea recedes.

linksman If you want to sound like a real cornball, call yourself a *linksman* instead of a golfer. It might impress your mother-in-law.

lip The edge of the hole is called the *lip*. If a putt stops short and is dangling over the edge of the hole, you would say, "It's hanging on the &*$% lip."

lip-out Any putt that hits a portion of the hole and spins out, failing to fall in, is a *lip-out*.

Nancy Lopez grimaces over her lip-out.

lithium balata A synthetic mix of materials used to cover some modern golf balls.

Little Ben Tour player Ben Crenshaw's nickname for his putter.

lizard killer A shot that flies very close to the ground—close enough to scare the lizards if doesn't kill them.

Liz Taylor If you hit a shot that's a little fat (see *fat*) but not too bad, that's a *Liz Taylor*. The term alludes to the, er, plumpness of the silver screen star.

load When the shaft of your club flexes (see *flex*) in the backswing, it is actually storing up energy that will be released in the downswing. The shaft is said to be *loading* when it stores up the power.

lob shot A *lob shot* is any shot that you play high into the air with the intention of it carrying only a short distance and landing softly.

lob wedge A club designed specifically to make lob shots easier to play, the *lob wedge* eliminates the player's need to make adjustments due to the lob wedge's excessive loft, which can range anywhere from 60 to 64 degrees.

local rules Certain courses or circumstances dictate that special *local rules* be adopted for play. These rules are not a part of the basic Rules of Golf but are allowed for within the rules. However, no penalty assessed by the Rules of Golf may be waived in favor of a local rule.

locker room The room at a golf club where you change your shoes, hang your hat, comb your hair with Barbacide, and do just about anything else you do in preparation or during the aftermath of a round of golf—except drink, which you do in the grillroom (see *grillroom*).

loft The *loft* of the club is the property that lifts the ball into the air. It's the angle at which the clubface leans away from the target. Also, when you hit a ball high into the air, you could say you played a *lofted* shot. Any club designed to hit such a shot, roughly from the seven-iron through the wedges, can be called a *lofted* club.

lofting iron A dated term for a club used to hit short, high approach shots onto a green.

long When you bust a long drive, your friends might say, "That's *long*." If you do this on a consistent basis, they might use *long* to describe your game in general.

There's a downside to long, however. If you hit a shot or a putt that travels farther than you expected, you might shake your head and say in disgust, "That's long."

long and wrong Suppose you're capable of hitting the ball immense distances but you very seldom hit it straight and never have any idea where it might go. If that's the case, the caddies would say you're *long and wrong*.

long ball A *long ball* can be a single shot that carries a tremendous distance or it can describe the longer shots in general. For example, "He plays the *long ball* extremely well."

long drive contest The carnival act of golf a *long drive contest* is a competition, the winner of which hits the ball the farthest distance.

long-driving A manner of describing someone who hits the ball a long way, for example, "Long-driving Al Falfa is among the best players at Swamp Lake CC."

long irons The irons with the least amount of loft are known collectively as the *long irons*. There is no set guideline for which clubs make up the long irons, but it's safe to say the long irons consist of the one-iron through four-iron.

long putter Putting is the first part of your game to go south on you as you become, ahem, more mature. In the mid-1980s, a bunch of players on the Senior Tour (see *Senior PGA Tour*) began using putters with extended shafts, which reached up to the middle of the chest. Such putters were dubbed *long putters* (pretty clever, those pro golfers, heh?). The long put-

STAN BADZ/PGA TOUR

V.J. Singh uses a long putter.

ter and the stroke it required eliminated the need for steady hands. Charlie Owens was the first player to use a long putter on a regular basis.

looked up What your idiot friends will say you did after you top (see *top*) a shot. Don't ever say this to anyone because it's the single most ridiculous piece of advice in the game. Your head should stay steady, but you're supposed to look up when you swing—in fact your right shoulder should turn your head forward on the follow-through.

loop A caddie refers to his round as a *loop* and sometimes refers to himself as a *looper*. The best caddies at a club are sometimes called *super loopers*. Unless you're the caddie, don't call your round a loop or your caddie a looper. Only the caddies are allowed to use these terms. It is okay, however, to call your caddie a super looper.

Loop, the The holes at the Old Course (see *Old Course*) that combine to change the direction of the course back toward the clubhouse.

loopy A swing that has movements that take the club off plane is described as *loopy*. The swings of Lee Trevino and Raymond Floyd are considered loopy.

loose impediments Anything that is produced by nature—twigs, loose flower petals, small stones, goose dung—is a *loose impediment* and may be moved from the area. You can move a loose impediment if its around your ball or in the line of your putt as long as you don't cause the ball to move. If the impediment has roots—grass or weeds—it's not a loose impediment. Sand and loose soil are only considered loose impediments on the green.

Lopez, Nancy One of the most beloved players in the history of women's golf, Nancy Lopez has won (as of this writing) 47 LPGA events, including 17 her first two years on tour, and a record five in a row. She has won three LPGA Championships and three Vare Trophies (see *Vare Trophy*) and is a four-time LPGA Player of the Year. The trademark of her game is her deft putting touch, of which Curtis Strange once said, "There's not a better putter alive, man, woman, or child." Her other trademarks: a swing so slow you could time a marathon by it and a smile so big you can see it from miles away.

Nancy Lopez in 1980.

UPI/CORBIS-BETTMANN

lost ball If you can't find your ball, it's lost. You have two options: Go back to the place you hit it from and hit another one, under penalty of one stroke (actually two, since you have to count the original ball, too—though the actual penalty is only one stroke), or pay to have a picture of your ball and an 800 phone number put on the side of milk cartons. That way somebody can call you if they find it.

lot of game An excellent player is sometimes said to have a *lot of game*.

low and slow One of the most popular swing keys (see *swing key*) is the backswing cue *low and slow*. It is a suggestion to take the club back from the ball slowly and low along the ground in order to establish proper tempo.

low-ball hitter A player who hits the ball consistently on a low trajectory is known as a *low-ball hitter*.

low gross A gross score is a player's score before handicap strokes are deducted. In tournament play, the player who shoots the best true score of the day is said to be *low gross*.

low side The *low side* of the hole is the point on the circumference of the hole opposite the direction from which an approaching ball breaks (see *break*).

LPGA The Ladies Professional Golfers Association. The series of events conducted by this organization is known as the *LPGA Tour*.

lunge A player who leans his body toward the ball at impact as opposed to turning his body through the ball is said to *lunge* at the ball. You don't want to do this.

L wedge A wedge with 60 degrees or more of loft used for playing very short, very high shots.

M

MacKenzie green Alternate name for a false green (see *false green*), so called because Dr. Alistair MacKenzie introduced this element of course architecture.

Magnolia Lane The most prestigious address in the game, Magnolia Lane is the driveway to the Augusta National Golf Club. It is named for the trees that line both sides of the pavement.

major championship There are four *major championships* in golf: the Masters, the U.S. Open, the British Open, and the PGA Championship. The word *major* is used to distinguish them from other professional golf tournaments. In conversation, you should simply refer to these four events as *the majors*.

major setup The major championships are played at courses considered among the most challenging in the world, which are prepared in a manner suited to test the world's best players. This course preparation is known as a *major setup* and results in such things as extremely hard, fast greens and, with the notable exception of the Masters, narrow fairways and deep rough.

make   There are two things in golf you sometimes need to make: a putt and a specific score on a hole. You might say of a certain putt, "I need to *make* this to tie," which means you need to hole the putt to tie your opponent on the hole. Also, in professional tournament play, the announcers may say, "Walsh needs to *make* four at the fifteenth in order to stay in the hunt." This means that, in the estimation of the speaker, the player must make a score of four on that hole to keep pace with the lead.

makeable   A putt or chip which has a realistic chance of being holed is described as *makeable*. That doesn't mean you will or should make it. It just means there's a good chance you might make it.

make the cut   See *cut*.

make the turn   When you finish the ninth hole and move on to the tenth, you've *made the turn* from the front side of the course to the back side.

making a move   In tournament play when a player begins to make scores that push him toward the leaders, he is said to be *making a move*.

mallet putter   A putter designed with a bigger, heavier clubhead than a blade putter.

manage his game well   When a player is said to *manage his game well*, it means he knows his strengths and weaknesses and does not try to play beyond his capabilities. It also means he recognizes how the course he's playing will affect his strengths and weaknesses.

Maniac Hill   Nickname for the practice range at Pinehurst Country Club (see *Pinehurst Country Club*).

mark   On the putting green, you are permitted to place a *mark* behind your ball and lift it. The act of doing so is called *marking* the ball. Also, the item placed behind the ball—a coin or small plastic disc—is know as a *mark* or a *marker*.

marker   There are three types of *markers* in golf. The first is the coin or other small item you place behind your ball on the putting green before lifting it. The second *markers* are the two objects placed on the teeing ground, from between which the tee shot must be played. The third type of *marker* is actually a person. When an odd number of players qualify for the final two rounds of tournament play, the first player off in the morning (the player in last position) might end up *sans* fellow competitors. In such a case, a capable player is given the job of playing along to give the player a feeling of the pace of tournament play and to keep his score. The person handling this task is a *marker.*

mark it What you say when you would like someone to mark his ball on the putting green so your putt won't hit his ball (see *mark*).

marshal At tournaments attended by spectators, a *marshal* is a volunteer who helps to control crowd movement about the course.

mashie When clubs had names, the five-iron was known as a *mashie.*

mashie-niblick The name for a club that had the loft of a six- or seven-iron.

Masters, the First played in 1934, the Masters is an invitational tournament contested each April at the Augusta National Golf Club in Augusta, Georgia. The club and the event were founded by the legendary amateur Bobby Jones. The tournament is unique in that it is organized and run by the club, so despite the fact that it is a very public event, it is also a very private event. The first of the four major championships in a given year, it is considered by golf aficionados to signal the beginning of the new year in golf. The Masters winner is awarded a green jacket, and no one has won more of them than Jack Nicklaus, six-time Masters champion.

master professional A PGA professional is considered a *master professional* upon completing certain requirements set forth by the PGA of America.

mat The rubber or artificial grass surface you hit off of at a driving range is called a *mat.*

match A *match* is a contest of match play between two players or two teams made up of two players (see *match play*). Also, a group competing in this manner is known as a *match.*

match cards In stroke play events, a common form of settling ties is to *match cards.* To do so, the players in question match their scorecards beginning from the first hole as if they had been playing a match play event. The first player to win a hole outright wins the matching of cards. Also, when two players playing in different groups wish to make a bet with each other, they might choose to *match cards* after the completion of the round as if they had played directly against each other for the full eighteen holes.

matched set A *matched set* of clubs is a set made by the same manufacturer and constructed to have a consistent progression of lofts, lies, lengths, and so on.

match play This is the original form of keeping score in golf and perhaps the most pure. In match play, the score is based on the number of holes won and lost as opposed to the total score. It is still the preferred manner of play for most non-tournament golfers and in nearly every betting game.

match player When a player, such as Lanny Wadkins, is spoken of in terms of his ability in match play competition, he is referred to as a *match player*. If someone suggests you are a good match player, it means they think you stand a better chance of winning at match play than you would at stroke play.

SAM GREENWOOD/PGA TOUR

Match player Lanny Wadkins.

match play tough A competitor who is considered very difficult to beat at match play is considered *match play tough*.

meat-and-potatoes par four A par-four hole that is long and straightforward, devoid of significant hazards other than greenside bunkers, is a real *meat-and-potatoes par four*—the hole is substantial but lacking in surprises.

medal A prize that members of a club compete for at stroke play. Often, such an event is held in the spring and known as the *spring medal*.

medalist To qualify for certain match play competitions, a player must first qualify for the competition by shooting certain scores in stroke play. The player who shoots the lowest scores during this qualifying is dubbed the *medalist* since traditionally he would receive some type of medal for his accomplishment.

medal play *Medal play* is the same thing as stroke play (see *stroke play*), the outcome being determined by the total number of strokes taken by players over the course of a round or rounds.

media tent At some tournaments, the pressroom (see *pressroom*) is actually a large tent, hence *media tent*. The media tent is large so it can accommodate the average golf writer, who doesn't miss too many free meals.

members The people who belong to a golf club are its *members*.

member's bounce When a person who plays a course regularly gets a fortuitous bounce, it is said to be a *member's bounce*.

men's tees The set of tees at a golf course from which the average male golfer should play. (Also see *white tees*.)

mental error If you attempt to hit a shot you know you can't pull off, you've made a mental error. A *mental error* is pretty much any mistake in strategy you make while not actually hitting the ball.

Merion Golf Club One of the world's great courses, Merion, on Philadelphia's Main Line, has hosted numerous U.S. Opens and other important championships. It is most famous for being the site—at the eleventh hole—where Bobby Jones won the 1930 U.S. Amateur and completed his grand slam (see *grand slam*). It was also the place where Lee Trevino defeated Jack Nicklaus in a playoff for the 1971 U.S. Open, prompting Trevino to say, "I love Merion, and I don't even know her last name."

Merry Mex Nickname for Lee Trevino, winner of six major championships—a pair each of U.S. Opens, British Opens, and PGA Championships.

metal wood Golf's modern oxymoron, the term *metal wood* is kind of silly, particularly considering that nearly all the woods manufactured today are made of steel. The term *wood* had evolved to the point where it referred to the type of club, as opposed to the composition of the club, long before the introduction of metal woods into the golf mainstream in the early to mid-1980s. To make it easy on yourself, just call them woods—everyone will know what you're talking about. A few folks think it's a good idea to refer to these clubs as *metals*, which makes as much sense as referring to shoes made of leather as *leathers*.

Mickey Mouse course It's difficult to determine exactly what the famous cartoon mouse ever did to become synonymous with a less than quality product, but whatever the reason, a course lacking in challenge is known as a real *Mickey Mouse course.*

middle When the hole is cut in the center of the green, in terms of depth, you simply say "It's *middle,*" to describe its location.

middle city Hit it down the middle of the fairway and you're in *middle city.*

middle left If the hole is cut in the center of the green, in terms of depth, and toward the left side, the hole position is described as *middle left.*

middle right If the hole is cut in the middle of the green, in terms of depth, and toward the right side of the green, the hole position is described as *middle right.*

mid-irons The *mid-irons* are the irons with an intermediate amount of loft. Which clubs make up the *mid-irons* is not a law set in stone, but you're safe referring to the five-, six-, and seven-irons as the *mid-irons.*

mid-mashie Before three-irons were three-irons, they were called *mid-mashies.*

milk the grip A key to a relaxed stroke, be it with the putter or in a full swing, is to apply the proper amount of grip pressure without creating tension in the hands. One way to avoid tension is to *milk the grip,* or repeatedly tighten and loosen the hands on the grip of the club until you are ready to start the club back. A superb example of this is Ben Crenshaw as he prepares to hit a putt. Watch closely and learn from Ben.

milk the lead When a player is so far ahead in a tournament or a match that he need not worry about giving shots back to the field, he may decide to *milk the lead* by taking a conservative approach that will prevent him from incurring any disastrous scores.

milled putter A milled putter is a putter hewn from a solid block of steel as opposed to one made by pouring steel into a mold.

Miller, Johnny The winner of the 1973 U.S. Open (by shooting the lowest final round for a winner in Open history, a 63) and the 1976 British Open, Miller was the golden child of pro golf in the early 1970s. His propensity for winning early in the year, when tournaments were played in the desert, earned him the nickname the Desert Fox.

Johnny Miller in 1973..

AP/WIDE WORLD PHOTOS

military golf A variation of army golf (see *army golf*), *military golf* is a euphemism for very erratic play.

million-dollar swing A player with a swing that is the envy of all who witness it is said to have a *million-dollar swing*.

miniature golf Sometimes referred to as putt-putt golf or Tom Thumb golf, *miniature golf* is a game designed, for the most part, to entertain children. It is played over carpeted cement, usually with wooden rails along the sides of putting *holes* to prevent the ball from going too far off course. Typically, there are obstacles such as embankments or, the classic, a windmill.

minitour A professional tour that is considered golf's equivalent of the minor leagues in baseball. There are numerous *minitours*, and they serve as a proving ground for aspiring PGA and LPGA Tour players.

misclub When a shot comes up short or is played long simply because the player selected the wrong club, he has *misclubbed*.

mis-hit Anytime you hit a shot that doesn't squarely strike the center of the clubface, you've *mis-hit* the shot. This word is hyphenated here when other "mis words" aren't because it appears a bit, er, vulgar otherwise.

misread You line up your putt and think it's going to break two inches to the right. You hit the putt, and it breaks eight feet to the left. You *misread* it, pal—and you need glasses.

miss Any shot that isn't directly contacted on the center of the clubface can be described as a *miss*, i.e., you missed the center of the clubface.

missable A putt is *missable* when it is of such a distance that you cannot necessarily assume you will make it.

miss the cut When a tournament player fails to qualify for the final two rounds of play, he has *missed the cut* (see *cut*).

miss the globe When you hit a shot that is so far off line that neither you nor any other humans can believe their eyes, you might say, "That *missed the globe*," i.e., the shot was almost wide of the planet.

mixed foursome When a foursome has two men and two women playing in it, it's a *mixed foursome*.

Monday qualifying The minicompetition for a place in the field that used to take place on the Monday prior to PGA Tour events was known as the *Monday qualifying*.

Monday's children In the days before the all-exempt tour (see *all-exempt tour*), a significant number of berths were open for qualifying on the Monday preceding each PGA Tour event. The players who frequently competed in these qualifying rounds were called *Monday's children*.

money A player who is solid under pressure and always seems to come through in the clutch is *money*. You would say of such a player (or perhaps they would say of you), "He's *money*."

money leaders Professional tour players near the top of the money winnings for a year are known as the *money leaders*. Don't confuse them with money lenders—they throw nickels around like manhole covers.

money list For professional tour players, the *money list* compares their performances against those of their peers. It is the cumulative total of prize money over the course of a tour season.

money player A player who plays his best during betting matches is known as a *money player*.

monk out In some parts of the United States, a player whose ball is headed for the trees might yell, "*Monk out!*" This means he'd like there to be a monkey in the trees, and that monkey should be so kind as to throw his ball out onto the fairway.

monster A demanding course is frequently referred to as a *monster*. Ben Hogan popularized the phrase when, after winning the 1951 U.S. Open at Oakland Hills Country Club in suburban Detroit, he said, "I'm glad I brought this course—this monster—to its knees." Hogan's line became instantly immortal, and Oakland Hills is still referred to as the Monster.

mounding Humps, bumps, and hills artificially constructed and incorporated into the terrain of a golf course are referred to collectively as *mounding*. As an architect, Jack Nicklaus has been criticized for his excessive mounding.

move When you want to sound like a real golfer describing another player's swing, you might say he's got a *good move*. This is probably the coolest way of referring to the golf swing. Also, when you are trailing the lead in an event and you shoot a score that puts you in contention, you are said to have *made a move*, and while you're doing it, you're *making a move*.

If you would like someone to mark their ball on the green (see *mark*), you might ask them to *move it*, which means you'd like them to mark the ball and then move the mark in one direction or the other so it won't be in your line (see *line*). This is typically done by moving the mark the length of a clubhead. It's cool to remind the person to move the ball back after you've asked them to move it in the first place. The only thing you don't want to move is the ball while you're addressing it. If the ball does move, you've got a problem.

moving day In the typical four-round professional event, the competitors refer to Saturday (the third round) as *moving day*, the day when they attempt to distance themselves from the bulk of the field and into a position to win the event on the following day.

Mr. X Nickname for PGA Tour player Miller Barber, who competed from the 1960s through the 1980s.

muff When you hit a shot fat (see *fat*), you've *muffed* it.

Muirfield Golf Club Located in East Lothian, Scotland, Muirfield Golf Club is considered one of the sternest tests of championship golf in the world. It is a regular stop on the British Open rota (see *rota*). Muirfield has a bit of sand—165 bunkers. Perhaps even more significant, it is home to the world's oldest club of golfers, the Honourable Company of Edinburgh Golfers, which was formed in 1744.

mulligan It is not uncommon for a player to suffer a poor result with his first swing of the day from the first tee. The causes for this range from the common hangover to stiffness, but the cure is simple. Golf being a game of gentlemen, it is an accepted practice to allow a player to hit a second "first" tee shot of the day, this shot being known as a *mulligan*. Some players refer to a mulligan as a *mully*. In the grand scheme of things, no one is harmed, and only a true jerk would complain about such a reprieve for his fellow golfer, unless, of course, you're playing in a tournament where the field of contestants extends beyond your immediate group. Then a mulligan is a no-no. (Also see *breakfast ball*.)

muni course Short for municipal course, *muni* originally described courses run by local municipalities but now refers to all daily-fee courses with relatively modest green fees.

my man A caddie refers to the player he is caddying for as *my man*, particularly if "my man" is playing well.

N

nailed it When you feel as if you've hit a shot as well as you possibly could have, you've *nailed it*.

nails If you want to sound like a super cool golfer, refer to your golf shoes as your *nails*. It's a slang expression alluding to the spikes on the bottom of your shoes. Try this one next time you're late for your tee time: "Sorry I'm late, boys. I'll be right with you as soon as I slip into my nails."

Nassau Perhaps the most basic betting game in golf, *Nassau* is a three-part bet with the same dollar value attached to each of the three bets. The three bets are for the front nine, the back nine, and the total match. The name is derived from Nassau Country Club in New York, where the bet is thought to have originated.

nasty A bad shot, a bad lie, a difficult-to-deal-with break on a putt—anything bad is *nasty*.

National Amateur The U.S. Amateur is sometimes referred to as the *National Amateur*.

National Open The U.S. Open is sometimes referred to as the *National Open*.

nativity scene When a golfer falls to his knees in exasperation and looks toward the heavens after missing a critical putt, it's a real *nativity scene*. Kind of breaks your heart, doesn't it?

natural When you make a birdie without the aid of handicap strokes in a match where you or others are getting handicap strokes, that true birdie is as a *natural* birdie. To sound like a real golfer, you'd shorten *natural* to *natch*, and use it as follows: "I made a *natch* three at the fifteenth, and I needed it because Harvey was getting one (a handicap stroke) and he made a four."

nature boy If you hit a lot of shots into the trees, your pals might start calling you *nature boy* since you like to spend time in the woods with all of God's creatures, both great and small.

nature walk While you're poking around in the woods looking for your ball, your dear friends might say you're *on a nature walk*.

nearest relief *Nearest relief* means just what it says. When you're taking a drop (see *drop*), you have to go to the nearest point that would remove you from the circumstances that entitle you to relief (see *relief*).

neck The term *neck* is an alternative word for hosel (see *hosel*).

neck job If you contact the ball with the neck of the club (yikes!), you've hit a *neck job*.

needle When you enjoy verbally taunting your pals (with friends like you, who needs enemies), you're giving them the *needle*. Injecting the *needle* is an art form—you have to be careful or your victim may get upset with you.

needs postage A shot that flies over the green without ever touching it is called air mail (see *air mail*). When you see your buddy's ball flying over the green in such a manner, you can gleefully shout, "That sucker *needs postage*, baby!" Funny stuff.

Nelson, Byron One of the game's all-time great players, Nelson is best remembered for his streak of 11 consecutive tour victories in 1945—he won 18 overall for the year. His dominance over his fellow pros during this period earned him the nickname Lord Byron. Nelson won five major championships during his career and is generally acknowledged as the first tour player to make the switch from hickory-shafted clubs to steel shafts.

Byron Nelson in 1945.

UPI/CORBIS-BETTMANN

net Your *net* score is the score you have after handicap strokes are deducted for a hole or for the overall round (see *gross*).

neutral grip When the hands are placed on the club in a neutral position, neither hand is turned underneath the shaft.

never had a chance After a putt that doesn't come close to going in the hole—that never even threatens to do so—you might say, "It *never had a chance*."

never up, never in If you want to sound like a real golfer, you'll never, ever use this phrase. It's something really annoying people say after you leave a putt short of the hole.

niblick *Niblick* had a lot of uses back when clubs had names instead of numbers. It referred to a type of wood designed for playing shots from bad lies and also was the equivalent of a wedge and a nine-iron.

Nicklaus, Jack Unquestionably the finest championship golfer in history, he won 20 major championships during his career. No one else is even close to Nicklaus in this category (Bobby Jones is second with a total of 13 major championships). It's unlikely that Nicklaus's record will ever be seriously challenged. His awesome total includes: six Masters, five PGA Championships, four U.S. Opens, three British Opens, and two U.S. Amateurs. In addition, Nicklaus was the runner-up in majors 17 times. He is considered the greatest pressure player ever, and when he was in contention, other players feared him.

night golf Although not terribly popular, it is possible to play golf at night, or *night golf*. Few courses in the world are equipped with lights, but a more practical alternative is a golf ball that has a fluorescent stick inserted into its center. As you might imagine, such a ball doesn't perform very well. The game is hard enough in the daylight, so do yourself a favor and stick to playing when the sun is up.

nine When you don't have time to play a full 18-hole round, you might try to sneak in *nine,* or half a round. Also, after a full 18 and a few beers, you might feel like hitting a few more shots or losing a few more bucks, so you indicate that you'd like to play nine more holes by saying to your pals, "Let's play another *nine.*"

nine-iron An iron club with approximately 45 to 48 degrees of loft and a lie of 62 to 64 degrees.

nineteenth hole The bar or grillroom at a club or course is frequently referred to as the *nineteenth hole.*

90-degree rule A stipulation of motorized cart operation that requires the driver to cross the fairway in straight lines.

nip it When you attempt to hit an iron shot very cleanly, without taking a divot, you would say you are trying to *nip it.*

no brainer A bad shot that is the result of a lack of concentration or poor planning is a *no brainer.*

no card When you've played such a miserable round of golf that you don't wish your score to become a matter of public record, you would refuse to turn in your score for posting. This is known as *no card,* or *NC* for short.

no chance A phrase popularized by television analyst Bob Rosburg, *no chance* is what you have when you hit your ball into a position from which it will be difficult to play the next shot with any amount of effectiveness.

Norman, Greg Probably the only player to become internationally famous for his inability to win the big championships. Nonetheless, Greg Norman is one of the most popular players in the history of the game. He hits the ball a long, long way and is considered the longest consistently accurate driver in the history of the game. He wins lots of money and lots of not-so-major tournaments, and golf fans generally respond warmly to his presence. Despite his failure to con-

Greg Norman

SAM GREENWOOD/PGA TOUR

sistently come through in the big events, he has to be considered the most dominant player of his time—and his time is still in full gear as of this writing. Nicknamed the Great White Shark (he really does kind of look like one), Norman has won two British Opens and is capable of phenomenal scoring performances.

nose The toe of a wooden club is known as the *nose*.

not enough As your ball plunks into yet another bunker, you can mutter to yourself, *"Not enough,"* which means you hit a club with more loft than required for the distance.

nuked When you flat-out crunch one, it has been *nuked,* baby. *Nuke* is short for *nuclear,* which is generally regarded as a frightfully strong source of power.

number This is a versatile word in golf, its meaning dependent upon the circumstances in which it is used. Before a betting match starts, someone might ask you for your *number* if he wants to know your handicap.

After the round, someone might ask you what *sort of number* you shot. What they want to know is your score for the round.

If, after the round, you don't feel like telling anyone about the quadruple bogey you made at the eleventh hole, you might just say, "I made a *number* there." They'll know you screwed up the hole.

On the other hand, if you're playing in a stroke play event and you think you need to shoot a low score in the final round to win, you would say, "I need to shoot a *number* today."

O

Oakmont Country Club The host to more significant championships than you can shake a stick at, Oakmont Country Club in Oakmont, Pennsylvania (a suburb of Pittsburgh), is one of the most severe tests of golf in the world and has been since it opened for play in 1903. Noted for its huge, lightning fast greens, it was the site of the famous playoff for the 1962 U.S. Open between Arnold Palmer and Jack Nicklaus.

OB An abbreviation for out-of-bounds. Since you're a real golfer, you'll opt to use *OB* instead of the full phrase. If you're lucky, you won't have to use either.

OB stakes The white stakes in the ground indicating where out-of-bounds begins are *OB stakes*.

ocean course Any course that is situated alongside an ocean is an *ocean course*.

off When you're having a bad day on the course, you might say you're having an *off day* or that your game is *off*.

off line A shot that is off target is said to be *off line*.

offset A clubhead is *offset* when a crook or slight bend in the hosel places the head slightly behind the shaft of the club. Offset clubs are considered a type of game improvement club (see *game improvement club*), designed to help players who commonly slice the ball (see *slice*).

Old Course The Old Course at St. Andrews, Scotland, is considered the world's oldest golf course, and as such it is hallowed ground to golfers. One of the world's quirkiest courses, which simply adds to its charm, it is also on the British Open rota (see *rota*). The Old Course is the home course for the Royal and Ancient Golf Club of St. Andrews (R & A), the governing body of golf for most of the world except the

UPI/CORBIS-BETTMANN

The Old Course at St. Andrews, Scotland, is one of the oldest in the world.

United States and Mexico. The R & A clubhouse is situated directly behind the eighteenth green of the Old Course. To sound like a real golfer, you should always refer to the course only as the Old Course, never as St. Andrews. St. Andrews is the name of the town.

on Your game is *on* when you're playing well. Your ball is *on* when it is sitting upon the green. If you hit the green in two shots, you're *on* in two.

one-fifty marker The most common yardage marker in golf indicates a spot 150 yards from the center of the green. Such a marker is known as the *one-fifty marker*. The marker itself varies from course to course. It is often a plastic disc (typically white) inserted flat in the fairway, a white line painted across the cart paths, or a distinct tree or shrub that is the same on each hole. The one-fifty marker helps the player get his bearings, although much more precise yardages have become the norm in modern times.

one-iron An iron with approximately 17 degrees of loft and approximately 56 degrees of lie. The severe lack of loft makes it a very difficult club to hit. You know you're up against a player when he has a *one-iron* and he knows how to use it. Top level players use it for accuracy from the tee on tight driving holes.

one-piece takeaway When your arms and the club move away from the ball together without any hinging in your wrists, that's a *one-piece takeaway*. As Martha Stewart would say, "It's a good thing."

one point Two teams of two partners who are playing best ball (see *best ball*) are playing for *one point*, that is, only the two low balls count toward the match.

one-putt When you hole out on your first putt on a given green, that's a *one-putt*.

one-shotter An awkward and rather goofy way of referring to a par-three hole. Don't use it.

one up In match play when you take a lead of one hole, you are *one up*. When you win a match by a single hole, you've won *one up*. And if you have a psychological advantage over your opponent (for instance, you are a long-hitter and he is not), you might be said to have *one up* on him. That doesn't necessarily mean you're going to beat him, however.

one-wood If you're a complete dork, you may refer to your driver as a *one-wood*. Expect to draw looks of disbelief if you do so.

on fire There are just as many ways to describe a good round as there are ways to describe a bad round. One of the ways to describe a good round is to say you're *on fire*.

on line A shot that heads exactly where you aimed it is *on line*.

on the bubble In professional tournament golf, there is a cut (see *cut*) after two rounds. Prior to the completion of the second round, players attempt to speculate as to what score will establish the cutoff. A player who is right at that score, that is, a player who is at 144 when it appears the cut will be at 144, is said to be *on the bubble*. What does it mean? The cutoff score can be altered by a player who shoots a low score late in the day, thereby bursting the bubble and knocking those on the bubble out of the tournament.

on the clock In professional golf, players are expected to play at a pace that does not slow down the field. When a group is playing slowly, an official begins timing the individuals and the group as a whole. When this is happening, the players are *on the clock*. If they don't speed up after a few warnings, they'll be penalized for slow play.

on the screws In the days when woods were actually constructed of wood, they had a plastic insert in the center of the face, the purpose of which was to prevent the wood from deteriorating from constant impact. Some inserts, particularly those in persimmon woods, were held in with several small screws, the number of screws depending upon the make of the club. When a player would hit a solid drive that felt good, he'd say, "I hit it *on the screws*." It's still a good expression to use, even if there aren't any screws in your woods.

open Another of golf's multimeaning words. Your stance is said to be *open* if your feet, knees, hips, and shoulders are pointed left of your target. Also, if you draw your left foot back from the ball, your stance is *open*. You might set up in such a way if you intend to fade the ball (see *fade*), or you might accidentally set up this way and hit a slice (see *slice*).

Your clubface is *open* if at address or impact it is aimed right of your target. It can also be *open* during your swing if at any time the clubhead

rotates into a position that will cause it to be open at impact if left uncorrected.

Open, the Some people prefer to call the British Open simply the Open, a designation they feel sets the tournament apart from the U.S. Open. This bit of snobbery is based on the fact that the Open is the world's oldest golf championship and, in many ways, its most prestigious.

open the door When a player in the lead of a tournament makes a mistake or series of mistakes that allow his nearest competitors an opportunity to catch him, he has *opened the door* for those players.

option Under certain circumstances, a player is presented with a choice of how to proceed under the Rules of Golf. For example, after hitting a ball in the water, a player may drop where the original ball was played from or move closer to the water hazard and drop. This choice is known in golf as an *option*.

Order of Merit On the European PGA Tour, the money list is known as the *Order of Merit*. So European, isn't it?

order of play The *order of play* is the order in which players should play their shots, based on the fact that the player farthest from the hole should play first. On the tee, the order of play is determined by the scores on the preceding hole, the lowest scores going first.

Oscar Brown Slang for out-of-bounds. A good term to use to sound like a cool golfer.

OT When a match goes into extra holes or a stroke play tournament goes to sudden death, some players refer to it as *OT*, short for overtime, a term used to describe extra play in team sports.

others In professional tournament play, statistics are kept regarding the difficulty of each hole on the course throughout the tournament. Such a statistic is usually presented in terms of the total number each of eagles, birdies, pars, bogeys, and *others*, i.e., scores worse than bogey.

Ouimet, Francis One of the most significant people in the history of American golf, Ouimet defeated Harry Vardon and Ted Ray in a playoff for the 1913 U.S. Open, sparking widespread popularity of the game in the United States at a time when British players were thought to rule golf.

Francis Ouimet in 1935.

AP/WIDE WORLD PHOTOS

Ouimet won the U.S. Amateur the following year and again in 1931.

out-of-bounds *Out-of-bounds* is ground that is not considered part of the golf course and from which you are not permitted to play under the Rules of Golf. When you hit a ball out-of-bounds, you are obliged to play another ball from the spot of the original shot and tack two penalty strokes onto your score. Out-of-bounds is traditionally marked by white stakes or a white fence.

outside agency A rules term referring to outside forces (other than wind or rain but including. people) that may

147

cause the ball to move. If your ball is moved by an *outside agency*, it's time to pull out your Rules of Golf book.

outside-in swing A swing which, through impact, moves from outside an imaginary line going straight back from the ball to inside that line after impact.

over the top An expression that refers to the act of the club tipping forward of the shoulders, in relation to the ball, at the beginning of the downswing, typically the result of the upper body improperly taking the lead in initiating the downswing. If you come *over the top* in your swing, you've got big problems.

overclub When you select a club for a given shot that produces a longer shot than necessary, you have *overclubbed*.

overcooked it Hit a full shot, chip, pitch, or putt too hard (and, as a result, too far), and you've *overcooked it*.

overlapping grip A manner of placing the hands on the club wherein the right pinkie finger is placed directly on top of the left index finger. Sometimes referred to as the Vardon grip.

oversized clubhead A clubhead that is larger than what is considered traditional is referred to as an *oversized clubhead*. Oversized clubheads are considered a form of game improvement club (see *game improvement club*).

overspin A ball that is spinning toward the target is said to have *overspin*. Fact is, however, you have to contact the top half of the ball with the blade of an iron to put actual *overspin* on it—and you wouldn't like the results. Even putts skid along the ground briefly before they start to spin toward the hole.

P

pace This term would be used only to refer to a putt, and you would be speaking of the speed at which the putt was moving. A putt struck at the proper speed to give it a chance to go in is said to have *good pace*. Also, a player who swings with fine tempo is said to swing at a *nice pace*.

pace, the In tournament play, *the pace* is the score of the leaders in relation to par during play. The player or players in the lead are said to be *setting the pace* while those players trailing are *off the pace*. When a player in contention drops back from the lead, he is said to have *fallen off the pace*.

pace of play The *pace of play* is the amount of time it takes a group or the field in general to move around the course.

packing A caddie sometimes refers to the act of carrying the bag as *packing the bag*.

packing heat A player who is considered to be a long hitter of the ball might be said to be *packing heat*, a street reference to someone who carries a gun.

pairing The grouping of golfers playing together in a stroke competition.

They aren't always a pair (two), and they aren't partners, but they are a *pairing*. When a player is assigned to his group, he is said to be *paired* with the other players in the group.

pairings sheet At a tournament, spectators have access to listings of the player pairings. Such a listing is known as a *pairings sheet*.

Palmer, Arnold Depending upon whom you ask, Arnold Palmer invented the game of golf. Strictly speak-

Arnold Palmer

ing, of course, that is not true, but Palmer is credited with introducing the game of golf to the masses of the American people, due in large part to his undeniable charisma and his passionate style of play. Palmer may not be the greatest competitive golfer of all time (although he did win eight major championships), but he is certainly the most popular and beloved of all time.

par *Par* is the standard of play expected of the excellent player, as it pertains to a given hole and the entire course. It is established by taking the number of shots an excellent player would be expected to take to reach a green (one, two, or three, depending upon the length of the hole) and adding two strokes as the standard number of putts for that hole.

parallel A standard for measuring the length of a golfer's backswing, *parallel* refers to the clubshaft being parallel to the ground at the top of the backswing. This position is deemed to be the perfect length for a controlled swing with the driver, but the fact is it's actually irrelevant to the quality of the swing. A swing that moves beyond this position is said to be *past parallel*.

parkland course In essence, any inland course that is laid out through woodsy, grassy, and generally flat terrain.

par three, par four, par five The three basic types of individual holes in golf, so called because of the number of shots in which an expert player should expect to play them.

partner When you play united with another player versus another team of two players, you are *partners* with the former. That's all it means—don't use it in any other sense.

pause at the top In a swing with nice tempo, there is a moment at the top of the player's swing in which the club is moving neither back nor down—it is motionless for just a split second, giving the lower body a chance to begin its downward motion. This moment of suspended animation is the *pause at the top*. You can see it expertly exaggerated in the swing of Nancy Lopez or Bob Murphy.

pass at it, make a good A player who has a technically sound swing is said to *make a good pass at it*—it, of course, being the ball.

Pebble Beach The most famous public-access course in America, rivaling Augusta National as the best

The seascape views at Pebble Beach (here from the eighteenth green) are legendary.

known course period, Pebble Beach is known for its astounding seaside vistas—many of the holes are along the cliffs of the California coastline. Pebble Beach is also the name of the town on the famed Monterey Peninsula, which the course calls home. As of this writing, Pebble Beach has hosted three U.S. Opens, (1972, 1982, and 1992), and it was the site of Tom Watson's dramatic seventeenth hole chip-in during the final round of the 1982 Open, which was the impetus of his victory over Jack Nicklaus. Pebble (as nearly everyone calls it) is also the home to the most famous pro-am in the world (see *pro-am*), the tournament founded by Bing Crosby and for years known simply as the Crosby. The event is now sponsored by AT&T.

peg *Peg* is slang for a wooden tee upon which the ball is perched in preparation for most tee shots. If you want to sound like someone who has been around the game all his life, use *peg* in place of *tee*.

penal A philosophy of golf course design that emphasizes the severe punishment of poorly played shots.

penalty When a player violates one of the numerous Rules of Golf, he is assessed a *penalty*. In stroke play, penalties are typically assessed in strokes (*penalty strokes*), with the most severe penalty being disqualification from the event for a major rules infraction. In match play, the typical penalty is loss of the hole on which the penalty occurs.

pencil bag A small carry bag is sometimes referred to as a *pencil bag* because it is very thin.

pencil hockey A player who cheats by writing in false scores or changing scores is said to be *playing pencil hockey*. You typically say this before you throw the person into a nearby lake.

pendulum stroke A putting stroke that keeps the wrists motionless (except for a smidge of movement created by the weight of the putter) and relies on the back and forth motion of the arms is a *pendulum stroke*—the motion of the arms resembles that of a pendulum.

perimeter-weighted irons An iron design that concentrates the bulk of the weight around the perimeter of the clubhead. Such designs help produce acceptable results from off-center hits. (See *cavity back*).

persimmon wood When woods were actually made of wood, the premier type of wood for such clubs was from the persimmon tree. *Persimmon wood* is exceptionally hard and also quite beautiful. A club made from persimmon is also referred to as a *persimmon wood*.

PGA Championship One of the game's four major championships, the PGA Championship, usually played in August, is typically the final of the four in a given calendar year. The tournament is considered the least prestigious of the big four, but it's still a major. Through 1957, the PGA Championship was conducted at match play, which made it unique among the majors. The switch to stroke play was made to accommodate television and to avoid the possibility of two no-name players competing for the championship.

PGA of America The national organization of golf professionals. This organization services its members and conducts the PGA Championship and, in conjunction with the British PGA, the Ryder Cup (see *Ryder Cup*).

PGA professional There is an important distinction between a PGA professional and a professional golfer. A person who calls himself a *PGA professional* is a member of the PGA of America and is, in all likelihood, in the business of servicing golfers. A professional golfer plays tournament golf for a living.

PGA Tour The organization of professional golfers and the series of events it conducts. The PGA Tour is responsible for the bulk of men's professional events in the United States, with the exception of the Masters (which is conducted by the Augusta National Golf Club) and the U.S. Open (conducted by the USGA—see *United States Golf Association*). The flagship event of the PGA Tour is the Players Championship (see *Players Championship*).

Phi Beta Caddie A club caddie who is noted for his knowledge of the game and of the course at which he caddies is sometimes called a *Phi Beta Caddie.*

picked up a pair If you're playing a high-low match (see *high-low*) and you and your partner both win a point, you've *picked up a pair* of points. On the next tee, you might say to your partner, "We picked up a pair there," dropping the specific reference to points. Also, in stroke play

when circumstances allow a contender to gain two shots on the leader, he is sometimes said to have *picked up a pair*.

picker A *picker* is a player who generally contacts his iron shots very cleanly, with little or no contact with the ground—the club simply clips the top of the grass. Tom Watson would be an example of a picker. The opposite of a picker is a digger (see *digger*).

pick it *Pick it* refers to striking the ball cleanly with the club making little or no contact with the ground. Here are some situations when you might decide to pick it: when a ball is sitting on top of the grass in the rough, creating the possibility of the club passing underneath the ball without making clean contact; under very wet conditions when the ground is soft and large divots make controlling the ball difficult; from a fairway bunker when the club digging into the sand interferes with clean contact; from wet sand, even near the green, when the club might bounce off the sand instead of digging into it, as is desirable for short bunker shots.

pick it up The phrase *pick it up* refers to the act of picking up the ball before play is completed for a given hole. You might decide to *pick it up* if you feel as if you're going to lose the hole or if your poor play on the hole is slowing up your group. Alternately, you might say to your opponent, *"Pick it up,"* to indicate that you are conceding a putt or the entire hole.

pick up To p*ick up* means to take your ball out of play with the intention of conceding the hole to your opponent or of not continuing on in stroke play.

piece of it, got a On the green, when the ball touches the hole but does not drop in, you *got a piece of it*—*it* in this case being the hole.

pigeon A pigeon is what a con man would call an easy mark. In golf betting parlance, a *pigeon* is someone easily defeated in a money match, in other words, a sucker.

pill Slang term for ball. This is a good one to use if you want to sound like you know what you're talking about. You might wow the boys by saying something such as, "I was knocking the snot out of that *pill* today."

pimple An alternate word for dimple (see *dimple*). A good term to use if you want to sound like a hayseed.

pin Specifically, the flagstick. However, the term is more commonly used to describe the location of the hole. If you say, "The *pin* is back," what you mean is the hole is cut in the rear of the green. Since the *pin* is placed in the hole, using the term to refer to the hole is commonplace.

pinch A chip shot is *pinched* when it is played with a short, crisp stroke with little or no follow-through.

Pinehurst Country Club The place where the notion of a golf resort was perfected, Pinehurst Hotel and Resort was laid out in the 1890s by Frederick Law Olmstead, the designer of New York's Central Park. Located in the Sandhills of North Carolina, Pinehurst Country Club is home to several golf courses, the most famous of which is the Number Two course, which was designed and steadfastly watched over by Donald Ross, the legendary architect from Dornoch, Scotland, (site of one of the world's great links courses) who grew to call Pinehurst home. Pinehurst Number Two is considered Ross's masterpiece.

Pine Valley Golf Club By just about any set of standards, Pine Valley, in Clementon, New Jersey, is the finest golf course in the world. Built in 1926 by Philadelphia hotelier George Crump, it introduced the idea of target golf. Technically, Pine Valley Golf Club is considered a borough unto itself and is in the hamlet of Pine Valley. If you're looking for it, don't ask someone where the town of Pine Valley is because they won't know what the heck you're talking about. Instead, look for the roller coaster at the Clementon Amusement Park. The club is right behind the roller coaster.

pin high When your ball is parallel with the hole, even if it's not on the green, it is *pin high*.

pin placement The exact location of the hole is sometimes referred to as the *pin placement*. Most greens are designed to allow for a variety of pin placements, so the hole location can be changed from day to day to maintain the challenge and level of interest for people who frequently play the same course.

pin position An alternative phrase for *pin placement*.

pinsetter The person who cuts the new hole each day and plugs the old hole is known as a *pinsetter*. While performing the task, the person is *pinsetting*.

pin sheet In tournament play, the competitors are given a diagram of each green on the course each round, the purpose of which is to show the location of the hole. The diagram is known as a *pin sheet*. Typically, a *pin sheet* gives the distance of the hole on the green in relation to the front of the green and from the side of the green nearest the hole.

pipeliner A tee shot straight down the center of the fairway is sometimes called a *pipeliner* because on some golf courses irrigation pipes are buried beneath the center of the fairway. Due to erosion over time, a bit of a dip in the ground over top of the pipe sometimes becomes noticeable for a portion of or the entire length of the fairway. *Pipeliner* is often shortened to *piped*, as in, "I really *piped* that one."

pistol grip A type of rubber or leather grip for a putter (the only club allowed to have a noncircular grip) that is flat on the top and larger at the butt end than a typical putting grip.

pit Some golfers refer to bunkers as *pits*. Sounds a bit more menacing.

pitch A *pitch* is a high-lofted, short shot typically played with the intention of the ball hitting the green softly. It is also the act of hitting such a shot. A *pitch* is different from a chip (see *chip*) because its trajectory is higher than that of a chip. Also, the swing made to produce the shot has a follow-through, while the miniswing for a chip stops at the ball.

pitch-and-putt An undersized golf course with short holes that can be played with just a wedge and a putter. *Pitch-and-putt* courses are often lighted for night play so boring, cheap guys can take their ugly girlfriends out where no one will see them.

Also, *pitch-and-putt* can be used in a derogatory sense to describe a regular golf course if you feel that the course is too easy and lacks sufficient length to be challenging.

pitch-and-run Different from a normal pitch shot (see *pitch*), a *pitch-and-run* is played with the intention of the ball running quite a bit when it hits the ground, and, as a result, it does not achieve (nor aspire to achieve) the trajectory of a typical pitch shot. The circumstances under which a pitch-and-run is played vary greatly, but it is considered essential for playing golf in Great Britain, where frequent high winds sometimes make it advisable to play the ball lower and along the ground as much as possible.

pitch-in When you play a pitch shot and—Shazam!—it goes in the hole, that's a *pitch-in*, mate.

pitching irons Collectively, the wedges in a set are sometimes referred to as the *pitching irons*, although the last time anyone spoke of them as such was during the Taft administration.

pitching wedge An iron club with approximately 50 to 52 degrees of loft and 63 to 65 degrees of lie. The *pitching wedge* is designed primarily for playing lofted shots from the grass.

pitch mark The indentation your approach shot makes in the green is a *pitch mark*. Make sure you fix it.

Pittsburgh Persimmon A nickname for metal woods, coined by the Taylor Made Golf Company when it introduced metal woods into the golf mainstream in the mid-1980s.

pivot When you turn your body away from the ball in the backswing, you are *pivoting* around your right leg, which remains firm and basically motionless until the start of the downswing.

placement The act of determining where you think a shot should land and stop and the actual striking of that shot is referred to as *placement* or *shot placement*. Typically, you would hear this used to compliment a player who thinks his way around the golf course.

For example, "His shot placement was terrific today. He hit the ball exactly where he wanted to on every green."

plate Yardage markers that are embedded into the ground are often referred to as *yardage plates* or simply *plates*. To sound like a real golfer you would just say *plate*, usually to ask a question such as, "Is there a plate out here?" meaning you want to know if there's a yardage plate in the vicinity of where you are standing. Also, if someone asks you the distance of a particular shot, you might say, "The plate says 180" (the inquiring soul has 180 yards to the green) or "There's a plate right at your foot, you idiot."

plateaued Some greens are said to be *plateaued*, which just means they are elevated a bit above the fairway and are generally flat in nature.

play In a broad sense, you *play* anytime you tee it up, hit it, find it, and hit it again. Also, each shot you hit during the course of a round is *played*. It has also become common to refer to a shot in the past tense as a *play*, for instance, "He made a fine play into the tenth green," which means he hit good shot. You might choose to compliment your buddy's nice shot by saying, "Nice play." Also, if you're about to attempt a nifty piece of shotmaking (see *shotmaker*), you might say something to your caddie such as, "I'm going to *play* a little shot here." He'll know what you mean.

Once you've made a stroke on the tee of a given hole, you're ball is said to be *in play* until you hole out on that hole. This means you're accountable for anything that happens to the ball while it's in play.

playability This term refers to the effectiveness, as determined by an individual, of a piece of equipment or a golf course. In other words, if you hit a particular driver and find it to your liking, you might say something such as, "It's got great *playability*," which means you hit it well. Also, a golf course is sometimes referred to in terms of its level of *playability*, which describes how appropriate the challenge is for players of various skill levels.

playable A ball is *playable* when it can be struck with a club. Typically, you would use this to describe a ball when you ascertain that you will be able to play a shot when moments before you were uncertain if that would be the case. For example, your pal might say to you as you're teetering on the brink of a pond, peering down at your ball,

"Hey, are you in the drink or what?" If you've decided that you can play a shot rather than take an unplayable lie (see *unplayable lie*), you might say, "It's in an alligator's mouth, but it's playable."

play club Before drivers were known as such, they were referred to as *play clubs*, a reference to the fact that on most holes the ball was put into play by striking it with this club.

play 'em down When you *play 'em down*, it means that you play the ball as you find it for every single shot during a round. No toe taps or nudges with your club to get a better lie. When you play 'em down, you're playing the game the way it was intended to be played.

player Believe it or not, not everyone who plays golf is a *player*. The term *player* is usually used to refer only to golfers of an extremely high skill level. For example, "He's a real player" means you like a guy's game and he probably just took twenty bucks from you.

Player, Gary One of the four men to have won each of the major championships at least once, Gary Player gained fame for his tenacity, physical fitness, and superb bunker play (among

Gary Player in 1996.

STAN BADZ/PGA TOUR

other things). Player won nine major championships from 1959 to 1978.

Players Championship Contested each March at the Tournament Players Club at Sawgrass, in Ponte Vedra, Florida, the *Players Championship* is the most prestigious event on the PGA Tour (remember, the Masters, U.S. and British Opens, and the PGA Championship aren't PGA Tour events). Some consider it a fifth major championship (see *major championship*).

playing easy When a course is prone to giving up a lot of low scores on a given day, it's *playing easy.*

playing fast When the ground is hard and the ball bounces more than normal, the course is *playing fast.*

playing hard When a course proves very difficult on a given day, resisting low scores, it's *playing hard.*

playing long When a course is wet and the ball is getting very little roll (see *roll*), it is *playing long.*

playing partner Another way of referring to your partner (see *partner*). Many people incorrectly use this term to describe the players who make up a pairing (see *pairing*) in stroke play.

playing professional A professional golfer who makes his livelihood by competing for prize money.

playing tough When a course doesn't yield many low scores on a given day, it is *playing tough.*

play it as it lies It means what it says, i.e., play the ball as you find it.

play it safe Golfers are often faced with a situation of having to choose between a risky shot that could be either hugely beneficial to them or damaging to their score, or a risk-free shot that eliminates much of the uncertainty. When you select the latter, you've decided to *play it safe.*

play off A dated term, to *play off* means to play a tee shot, particularly on the first hole of a round.

playoff When players are tied at the end of regulation play in a match or a tournament, the outcome of the match or event is settled by further play

Hale Irwin celebrates a birdie putt during his play-off showdown with Mike Donald at the 1990 U.S. Open.

called a *playoff*. Most playoffs are sudden death playoffs, wherein the first person to win a hole wins the match or event. The U.S. Open still clings to the archaic idea of an 18-hole playoff to settle ties. The British Open conducts a four- or five-hole mini-playoff at stroke play.

play off the low ball In a match where handicap strokes are being given, the number of strokes is determined by the difference between the low handicap in the group and each of the other handicaps. This is known as *playing off the low ball*. For example, if your handicap is four and the other three members in your group have handicaps of six, eight, and ten, the number of shots they receive is determined by subtracting your handicap from each of theirs, so the six handicap would receive two shots, and so forth. The player with the low handicap (the low ball) doesn't receive any strokes.

play out of turn When you hit your shot but you're not away (see *away*), you've *played out of turn*. It's a no-no in tournament play, but it's no big deal when you're playing on Saturday with Fred and Bill.

play through If the group behind your group is playing faster than you,

it's a point of etiquette that you should stand aside and let them *play through*.

plug When your ball embeds in the ground, it has *plugged*.

plumb bob A method some players use to determine the general lay of the land on the putting green, it involves holding the butt end of the club between two fingers and letting the weight of the clubhead act much like a lead weight *plumb bob* on the end of string. The shaft of the club acts as a point of reference for the player. Frankly, even players that do this aren't exactly sure why they do it.

AP/WIDE WORLD PHOTOS

Mickey Wright uses her club as a plumb bob to size up the green.

plus fours *Plus fours* were pants tailored specifically for golf in the 1920s and 1930s with legs four inches longer than standard sporting knickerbockers so that they would drop below the knee and not impair the player's swinging action.

plus handicap One of the cruelest things in golf is that a player who consistently betters par not only doesn't get handicap strokes deducted from his score but must add strokes to his score. Such a handicap is a *plus handicap*, and if you're unfortunate enough to be one of the few people so afflicted, you're a *plus man*. If it works out that you typically have to add five shots to your score, your handicap is a *plus five*.

Poa annua A weed that sometimes overgrows the grass on greens and fairways. In moist climates, *Poa annua* can be an excellent putting surface as long as the entire green consists of it.

point A *point* refers to the number of betting units available on a given hole. Most matches involving two teams of two players are worth either one or two points per hole as the basic bet, but a hole can become much more valuable due to carryovers (see *carryover*).

poke-and-hope A shot played out from trees or through trees, with luck being the primary factor in determining the fate of the shot.

poly A betting game in which any holed putt longer than the length of the flagstick (the pole) earns the player a point.

pond ball Some players carry old golf balls in their bags for use on holes with water hazards, the idea being to avoid losing a new (and expensive) ball in the water. Any ball earmarked for such use by a player is called a *pond ball*.

pop Sometimes short putts are said to be popped into the hole. For example, if you wanted to hole out a short putt rather than mark it, you might say, "Just let me *pop* this in real quick."

pop stroke A style of putting that emphasizes use of the wrists with very little arm movement, the *pop stroke* was the preferred way of putting on the shaggy or inconsistent greens that were the norm before golf course maintenance became the advanced science it is today.

pop-up A shot that unintentionally flies excessively high and short, typically caused by too steep a downswing.

pose on it If you're like most golfers, you don't hit a whole bunch of great shots. So when you do, take a moment to savor and *pose on it*, i.e., hold your follow-through and gaze in admiration as your ball soars through the air.

position A A shot played to a point considered ideal for the subsequent shot is said to be in *position A*.

Postage Stamp Nickname for the short, par-three eighth hole at Royal Troon, one of the courses on the British Open rota (see *rota*).

post a score To *post a score* means to record the score for the record, i.e. enter it into the handicap computer. The term stems from the act of posting tournament scores on a leaderboard (see *leaderboard*) at professional events so that those in attendance can see how a player fared.

Also, in professional golf, a player who finishes early in the final round with a low score that moves him into contention is said to have *posted* whatever number he shot.

posture In golf, your *posture* refers to the angles you set with your body as you address the ball.

pot bunker A *pot bunker* is a deep bunker with a small circumference, the top of which is level with the general terrain. A *pot bunker* doesn't have a face (see *face*) as much as it has walls of equal height.

power hitter A *power hitter* is anyone who consistently hits the ball great distances.

power one If you were trying to describe the necessity to hit a long tee shot on a given hole, you might say that the hole requires a player to *power one* from the tee.

power outage A *power outage* occurs when a player who usually hits the ball a long way seems unable to do so on a given day, or when a player who is normally a fine player suddenly starts to play poorly.

practice green Most golf courses have a putting green that is not part of the actual course and that is intended as a practice area and a place for a player to become familiar with the speed and texture of the greens on the course. Such a green is referred to as a *practice green*.

practice range An area where players can hit warm-up shots prior to a round or practice their game at other times.

practice swing The idea behind a *practice swing* is to rehearse exactly, without striking the ball, the swing you'll need to make to hit an effective shot. If you take a practice swing before each shot, do the world a favor and limit it to one—practice swings (note the plural) slow down play and make you a nuisance.

practice tee The area at a golf course designed and laid out for practice shots is sometimes referred to as the *practice tee*.

preferred lie The lie of your ball, particularly if you're playing winter rules (see *winter rules*), after you've moved it is a *preferred lie*. You and your pals should all agree to play preferred lies before the start of a round. You can simply call this cheating if you're the only one in the group doing it.

pre-shot routine A *pre-shot routine* consists of anything a player does in preparation to play a shot up to the point at which he starts to swing the club. It cannot be clearly defined as it is different for each person, but it can include things such as a practice swing, target selection, and mental imagery.

president Only in golf would something such as the *president* have existed. It was a club with a hole in the face used to play shots out of the water.

press The primary meaning of this term relates to betting matches wherein a player or team, typically when two down, requests that a new match within the match be started at the point they declare the press. The *press* bet continues until the end of the match. Some players agree prior to a match that anytime a player or team falls two holes behind, a press is automatically applied. Such an agreement is called an *automatic two-down press* or *automatic*.

A secondary meaning refers to the idea of trying too hard—*pressing*—and getting poor results. In this sense, it's short for pressure, which is self-induced.

pressroom At a professional golf tournament, the *pressroom* is where writers hang out in the air-conditioning, eating free sandwiches and drinking free drinks and watching the event on television rather than stepping outside and actually witnessing it. A player who shoots a good score is paraded into a room where the writers interview him *en masse*, grilling the individual with tough questions such as, "What were you thinking as you stood on the tenth tee and found yourself in the lead?" and "What kind of courtesy car did you get this week? Is it an Olds?" Eventually, after eating more free sandwiches, the writers sit down and write stories about the day's events while the photographers mill around aimlessly complaining about the officials who won't let them stand in the bunkers with the players so they can click off a good photo.

pressure putt A *pressure putt* is any putt that has something riding on its outcome. It can be a putt to win a hole, win a match, win money, win a tournament, or win back your self-respect. Miss it and you're a choker (see *choke*). Make it and you're a star.

pretty An obsolete term referring to a fairway. Also, when someone hits a particularly good shot, you might whistle and say, "*Pretty.*"

primary rough A course set up for championship play often has two levels of rough. The *primary rough* is the really deep stuff.

Principal's Nose A bunker on the sixteenth hole at the Old Course (see *Old Course*).

pro Short for professional golfer or golf professional. When someone refers to *the pros*, he's usually referring collectively to professional tour players. When the reference is to *the pro*, it typically means a golf professional.

pro-am Short for professional-amateur, it's a format of play that teams a professional golfer with one or more amateurs.

professional golfer Unlike golf professionals (club pros), the *professional golfer* plays tournament golf for a living (see *golf professional*).

pronation Rotation of the arm and wrist so that the palm faces downward. You might hear people speak about the *pronation* of the left arm in the backswing. Some friendly advice: If you hear such a reference, run very quickly away from the person who said it and never again play with him. When you get home, call the Nerd Police.

pro side On the putting green, the high side (see *high side*) of the hole (the direction from which the ball is breaking toward the hole) is sometimes referred to as the *pro side*, due to the mistaken belief that professional golfers miss putts more frequently on that side of the hole.

pro tees Most golf courses have several sets of tee boxes. Those tees from which the course plays longest and/or most difficult are sometimes referred to as the *pro tees*. Other slang for these tees includes *blue tees*, *the blues*, *the tips*, and the *waybacks*.

provisional ball When you're uncertain as to the fate of your ball after playing a shot—maybe it went out-of-bounds, maybe it didn't—the Rules of Golf allow you to play a *provisional ball*, which will be put into play only if you're original ball is indeed out-of-bounds or lost or whatever. If you find your original ball and it's safe, you simply pick up the provisional ball. Here's a tip: Remember to tell the guys with whom you're playing, in a loud, clear voice, that you are playing a provisional ball. If you don't, whatever strokes you accumulate with it count.

public links Any golf course open to the paying public.

publinx Anything relating specifically to the playing of golf on public golf courses or to the course itself.

puddle jumper Any low-flying ball, almost always a mis-hit, that skips off the top of a water hazard and lands safely on the other side is a *puddle jumper*.

pull A shot that flies straight left of the target is a *pull*. A pull doesn't curve

like a hook (see *hook*). It flies straight and off-target.

pull cart A device with two small wheels, a stand for a golf bag, and a long handle, which can be pulled or pushed around so a player doesn't have to carry his bag.

pull-hook A *pull-hook* is a shot that starts out like a pull (flying on a straight line but left of the target) and evolves into a hook (a shot that curves from right to left).

punch shot A *punch shot* is an iron shot played with little or no follow-through, the idea being to minimize the trajectory of the shot. You might elect to play such a shot into a strong wind.

punch bowl green Any putting green set in a natural hollow is a *punch bowl green*. Shots played toward such a green tend to gather in the center.

puppy will hunt, that A phrase sometimes used to express delight with a long tee shot or any shot that appears destined to end up close to the hole. Use it in combination with a rebel yell or add the word *baby* for maximum effect.

pure A shot that is struck so well you can feel the sensation run up your arms and down to your toes is *pure*. When you hit one like this, you've *pured* it. Caution: Please don't ever tell anyone it felt better than sex. If you have to ask why, you might think about spending a little less time on the golf course.

purse The total amount of money to be divided up among the competitors in a professional event is the *purse*. The better a player does, the bigger his share of the *purse*.

push A shot that flies on a straight line but is right of the target.

put a tack on it If someone tells you to *put a tack on it,* it means they want you to mark your ball on the putting green.

puts a good move on the ball, he When a player has a good swing, it is not uncommon for people to say that *he puts a good move on the ball.*

putt A *putt* is any shot played along the ground on the putting green with the intention of placing the ball near or in the hole. It is also the act of striking such a shot. While you are striking the shot, you are said to be *putting*. Technically speaking, a ball has to lie on the putting green for the stroke played to be considered a putt. A shot played from off the green with a putter is just, well, a shot played from off the green with a putter. Still, you can say you putted the ball from off the green. Everyone will know what you're talking about.

putter A club with a minimal amount of loft designed for playing shots along the ground on the putting green. Also, the word *putter* is used when speaking of someone's skills in the putting area of the game, i.e., "He's a very fine *putter*."

putting contest A *putting contest* is just what it sounds like, a contest of putting skills spiced up with a wager, typically taking place on the practice green.

putting green The closely mown area where the hole is cut. Don't use this variation—simply refer to it as a green.

putt out When you elect to finish putting (hole out) even when you are no longer away, you have decided to *putt out*. It's okay to do so, just announce your intentions beforehand. And if you miss it, count it.

putt-putt An alternative term for miniature golf (see *miniature golf*).

putting surface An alternative term for green.

quacker Slang for a duck hook (see *duck hook*).

quail-high A low-flying shot is said to be *quail high*.

quarter shot A *quarter shot* is any shot played with a swing that is only one-quarter as long and powerful as a full shot. You would typically play a quarter shot with a wedge.

quick When the ball moves very quickly on the greens, the greens and the putts on them are said to be *quick*.

Also, when you *get a little quick* with your swing, it means your swing lacks tempo and timing, which results in a poor shot.

Q School Toward the end of each year, aspiring PGA Tour players play in a tournament known as *Q School*

AP/WIDE WORLD PHOTOS

Mac O'Grady, a 17-time Q School participant.

(short for Qualifying School). The top finishers at *Q School* earn their tour card (see *tour card*), which entitles them to compete on the PGA Tour the following year. Mac O'Grady has been to Q School 17 times.

R

R & A Abbreviation for the Royal and Ancient Golf Club of St. Andrews, Scotland, the governing body of golf throughout the world with the exception of the United States and Mexico.

rabbit The main usage of this term refers to a professional golfer who has no exemption (see *exemption*) and is forced to play qualifying rounds to make it into the field for a professional event.

Also, but less common, a *rabbit* is a player of little skill.

Rae's Creek A small stream that fronts the twelfth green at Augusta National Golf Club then turns and runs along the thirteenth fairway before cutting in front of the thirteenth green. It is the most devilish of the great course's hazards.

railroad tie Some older golf courses in Great Britain use *railroad ties* or wooden planking to reinforce the faces of bunkers. It became trendy in the late 1970s and 1980s to use railroad ties as an unnecessary architectural accessory to create a certain look American course developers liked. As such, railroad ties became the symbol of architectural excess and unnatural design—at least for people who care about such things.

rainmaker A shot that is popped up (see *pop-up*) or hit much higher than intended is sometimes referred to as a *rainmaker* because of the ball's vicinity to the clouds.

rake The tool provided on the course to smooth over the sand in bunkers is a *rake,* and when you use it, you're *raking* the bunker. Also, at one time, a club known as a *rake* was common. It had slots in the face that were thought to make the club effective for shots from water and sand.

rammed it A putt that is played aggressively toward the hole with more than ample speed is *rammed.* You might play such a putt because you are uncertain about a subtle break in the green and feel that the extra speed will eliminate the break. Or you might play such a putt because you're a lousy putter.

range Short for practice range or driving range. Also, a player who is an excellent putter from a particular distance would refer to that distance as his *range,* i.e., "Ten- to fifteen-foot putts are my range."

range balls The balls designated for use on a practice range are known as *range balls* and are typically painted with red stripes to indicate them as such (see *striper*).

ranger A golf course employee who typically roams the course in a motorized golf car, making sure that players are keeping up with the pace of play (see *pace of play*).

rap A firmly struck putt is said to have been given a good *rap.*

rattle it in When you *rattle it in,* the ball appears to ricochet off the interior wall of the hole before dropping to the bottom.

reachable When it is accepted knowledge that two excellent shots will get a player home (see *home*) on a par five or that the green can be driven on a par four, the holes are said to be *reachable.*

read When you assess the green as a whole or the line of a single putt as it relates to speed, direction, and texture of the grass, you are *reading* the green. If you feel you made a putt because of the read someone else (such as your caddie or partner) made for you, you'd say to them, "*Nice read,*" to indicate your appreciation.

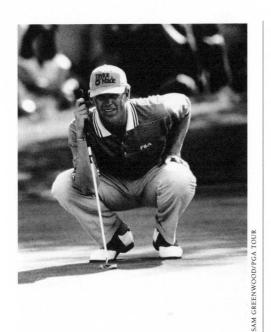

SAM GREENWOOD/PGA TOUR

Lee Janzen reads the green before a putt.

ready golf As the amount of time it takes to play a round of golf has increased, the patience of those who play the game has decreased. It is now considered practical in nontournament play for players to hit their shots whenever they are ready—*ready golf*—rather than waiting for honors (see *honor*) or waiting to see who is away (see *away*).

reality check A player who seems to have it all together one moment then suddenly hits a bad stretch of holes is said to be undergoing a *reality check*.

Similarly, in big-time tournament golf, a player who unexpectedly finds himself in the lead during the final round but begins to unravel as soon as he realizes it is having a reality check.

recovery Anytime you hit a shot from an undesirable position and play it to a desirable position—for example, you're in a bunker and play the ball onto the green—you've played a *recovery shot*. It's only a recovery shot if you successfully play to where you intended. If you fail to escape the bunker, it's just a bad shot.

Redan Hole A par three with a green set diagonal to the tee and slanted away, with a steep drop-off or swale off to one side of the green. The green positioning, the drop-off, and a bunker give the hole two lines of defense no matter where the hole is cut.

Red Grange A single-round score of 77, which was the uniform number of football's Red Grange, the famed Galloping Ghost. Grange was an all-American halfback at the University of Illinois in 1923 and 1924 before joining the Chicago Bears in 1925.

red numbers When you're in the *red numbers* you're under par. The term originated because red numbers were used on scoreboards to indicate under par scores.

red tees Traditionally, the women's tees on a golf course are designated by red tee markers, which led to them being called the *red tees*.

regrip Part of the lexicon of the golf swing, *regripping* occurs when a player temporarily loosens his grip at the top of the swing and then grabs tighter in preparation for the downswing. It's not a good thing, since it generally affects the angle of the clubface.

Also, you *regrip* your club when you put a new rubber or leather grip on the butt end of the shaft (see *grip*).

regular flex The shafts in golf clubs are rated on the amount that they flex or bend during the swing. The broad categories classifying this property are regular, stiff, and extra stiff. A regular shaft is usually coded with the single letter R.

regulation This term refers to a level of play that is considered standard for an expert player. A score of par for a hole or an entire round is sometimes referred to as a *regulation par* or a *regulation round*. Also, when your ball stops on the green in two shots less than par for a given hole, you are said to have hit the green *in regulation* or be on *in regulation*.

release One of the most convoluted terms in the game, *release* refers to a number of things. As it relates to your swing, *release* means that moment when the wrists finally uncock in the downswing, unleashing the clubhead toward the ball. The term is also used to describe the right side of the body's turn toward the ball in the downswing—*releasing* the right side. Also, some people use the term *release* to describe the action of the clubface squaring and then seemingly closing through impact.

An entirely different meaning for *release* describes the ball rolling once it hits the green, as opposed to immediately stopping. For the most part, *release* in this sense is used in a negative manner, i.e., when a ball hits the green and stops and the player wanted it to roll, he might say, "It didn't release." If you're friends don't already consider you a crybaby, frequently saying your ball didn't release is a good way to make them start.

relief Under certain Rules of Golf, you are allowed to pick up your ball and move it away from obstructions without incurring a penalty. When you elect to do so, you are *taking relief*. The rules that allow you to do so are said to *entitle you to relief*. To know when you can take relief and when you can't, check the rules.

reload After you hit a shot out-of-bounds, the Rules of Golf dictate that you must play another ball (with a penalty, of course) from the original spot. When you dip into your pocket or bag to get another ball, you might say, "I'm going to *reload*," to indicate that you're about to play another shot.

repeating swing When you say of a player that he has a *repeating swing*, it means the swing is mechanically sound to the point that it can be reproduced shot after shot with little deviation.

repertoire [of shots] This word means the same outside of golf as it does in golf. Your *repertoire* of shots refers collectively to all the types of shots you are capable of playing with a modicum of proficiency.

reroute If you've ever wondered what that crazy move at the top of Ray Floyd's swing is, or that funky loop in Lee Trevino's swing, you can impress your pals by saying, "Floyd *reroutes* his club at the top. So does Trevino." What you mean is that the club does not move through the entire swing on the same plane (route).

resort golf *Resort golf* refers to the idea of a golf vacation, when the hotel you stay at also has a golf course. Originally, such hotel courses were very easy and with few hazards, the idea being that resort golf should be relaxing rather than a struggle.

reverse C A follow-through position in which the body loosely forms a *reverse C*. Once considered standard, this position is no longer espoused by swingologists due to the immense amount of strain it places on the back.

reverse overlap grip Perhaps the most common grip for putting, the *reverse overlap grip* places the left index finger over the first two or three fingers on the right hand, depending upon the player's preference.

reverse pivot Two of the ugliest words in golf, a *reverse pivot* is what occurs when you shift your weight toward the target in the backswing, as opposed to away from the target (the generally accepted technique).

ribbed A *ribbed* club features wide, deep grooves on the face. Such clubs are illegal.

rifle A long, straight, hard shot is said to be *rifled*.

right hand, too much Another of the great excuses to use when you don't want anyone to know what the hell you're talking about. No serious player would ever say "*too much right hand*" because there's no such thing. Players often use this phrase after they hit a hook or a pull (see *hook* and *pull*), thinking the clubface has closed through impact because they turned their right hand over top of the left hand. Chances are excellent, however, that your hook or pull was created long before your hands reached the impact zone (see *impact zone*). So if you need an excuse for a hook or a pull, only use this one when you're playing with guys who don't know jack about the golf swing.

right-to-left shot Any shot that, while in the air, curves from right to left is said to be a *right-to-left shot*.

right-to-right A slang expression for a shot that is extremely far right of the target, *right-to-right* is a play on the phrase *right-to-left shot*.

rim The *rim* is the outer edge of the hole. When a putt hits the edge of the hole but doesn't fall in, it is sometimes called a *rim out*.

ringer A *ringer* is a good player entered into an event field or betting match for the sole purpose of securing victory for the side on which (or for which) he is playing. The term in this sense dates back to the fifteenth century when it meant someone who was a fake or a fraud—perhaps someone who, in those long ago days, entered an archery competition under false pretense. Today, you'd use this expression in more of a joking manner, i.e., if someone is playing exceptionally well the first time you play with them, you might refer to them as a ringer.

ringer score If you took the best score you've ever had on each of the holes on the course you frequently play and added them up, the total would be your *ringer score* for that course. For example, if the best score you ever made on the first hole was a three, the best score you ever made on the second hole was a four, the best score you ever made on the third hole was two, and so on, you would add these and tally up your ringer score. Why is it called a ringer score? It's hard to keep track of things after awhile, so when people silly enough to keep such a score make a score they believe belongs in their *ringer* total, they draw a circle or ring around the number on their scorecard then compare the figure to their ringer score when they get home. If you do keep a ringer score, don't admit to it under any circumstances unless you enjoy being laughed at.

rinse When your ball splashes into a water hazard, it's *taking a rinse*. When you put your ball into a ball washer, you're *giving it a rinse*. When you have a beer during or after a round, you're *having a rinse*.

ripped When you hit a shot a long, long way, you've *ripped* it.

risk reward An architectural philosophy that leans toward the building of holes that require a player to play a risky shot in order to get the best possible result (the reward).

Road Hole The most demanding par four in championship golf is the seventeenth hole at the Old Course, St. Andrews, Scotland—the *Road Hole*. The hole is so named for a small (but very much in play) road (more like a footpath) located directly behind the green and bordered by a wall, which is also in play. The Road Hole was the site of Tom Watson's demise in the 1984 British Open when his second shot went over the green and onto the road, nestling close to the wall. Seve Ballesteros took the title and prevented Watson from matching Harry Vardon's record of six British Open victories.

robbed When you believe the golf gods have unjustly prevented a putt from falling, you might say, "I was *robbed*." It might make you feel better, but it won't make the ball topple into the hole.

rock Slang for golf ball, typically used to express admiration for a player's ability to hit the ball a long way, e.g., "Man, he can move that *rock*."

rock pile *Rock pile* is slang for the practice range and for any pile of practice balls.

roll Once a shot hits the ground, the *roll* is the distance it moves along the ground. Also, many players refer to a putt as a *roll*, and to the act of putting as *rolling it*, for example, "I was rolling it good today."

roller coaster round A round during which your scores are inconsistent—a real mix of good scores and bad scores—is a *roller coaster round* because your game is up and down all day.

roll it over When you improve your lie (see *improved lie*), you're *rolling it over*, *it* referring to the ball.

roll on it, put a good When you hit a good putt—even if doesn't go in (or especially when it doesn't go in)—you might say, "I *put a good roll on it*." It might make you feel better.

Ronstadt, a Singer Linda Ronstadt's most famous song was "Blue Bayou." When you crush a drive way past everyone in your group, you can say you hit a Ronstadt. When they ask you what you mean, you say, "I blew by you."

rope hook A hard, low-flying hook (see *hook*) is known as a *rope hook*. The expression is borrowed from baseball, where a hard-hit line drive is known as a frozen rope (see *frozen rope*).

ropes, the At a big-time competitive event, *the ropes* are, well, ropes that separate the spectators from the parts of the course where the play is expected to be conducted. That's not to say that the pros never hit a shot to the wrong side of the ropes, it's just that they prefer to stay inside the ropes—where the action is.

rota Short for rotation, the *rota* refers to the list of courses that alternately host the British Open. The modern rota includes the Old Course, Muirfield, Royal Troon, Turnberry, Royal Lytham, and Royal Birkdale.

rotation The twisting motion of the arms during the swing is the *rotation*.

rough The part of the golf course that is not as closely mown as the fairway and is not a tee, green, or hazard is the *rough*.

round Once around the course, the full 18 holes, and you've played a *round* of golf.

routine par In golf, a *routine par* is typically anything but routine. The term is used to jokingly describe a par score on a hole when it appeared the player would make a much higher score. So if you chip in or hole a very long putt for par, you might grin and say, "Just a routine par, boys."

The term is sometimes used to describe a par score for a hole that actually is *routine,* in this sense meaning a green hit in regulation and two putts.

Royal and Ancient Golf Club It's not the oldest club of golfers in the world—that distinction goes to the Honourable Company of Edinburgh

Golfers—but it's the most famous. It serves as the ruling body for golf for the entire world except the United States and Mexico. The Royal and Ancient Golf Club runs the British Open (among other things) from its home in St. Andrews, Scotland. If you want to sound like you're knowledgeable, simply refer to this club as the Royal and Ancient or the R & A.

The Clubhouse at the R&A.

UPI/CORBIS-BETTMANN

rubber core ball The basic type of ball, which came into play around the turn of the century and is still used today, is known as a *rubber core ball* because it has a small, rubber ball at its center.

rub of the green Any time your ball takes a bad bounce or does something unexpected (and not to your advantage), you chalk it up to *rub of the green*. There's no relief under the Rules

of Golf for a bad bounce, but you can take comfort in the fact that rub of the green seems to be handed out in equal doses to all golfers.

Rules of Golf The *Rules of Golf*, written and administered by the USGA or the R&A, depending upon where you're playing (see *United States Golf Association* and *Royal and Ancient Golf Club*), are the rules of the game. They become more voluminous in nature each year. Technically speaking, you only need to abide by them in tournament competition, but it's a good idea to do so all the time.

run *Run* describes the action of the ball anytime it's bouncing or rolling along the ground. While the ball is doing so, it is said to be *running*.

run-up shot A low shot played with the intention of making the ball run up near the hole is a *run-up shot*. You can also refer to such a shot as a *runner*, which sounds better and will save you a breath or two.

rut iron When horse-drawn wagons commonly traversed golf courses, the wheels of the carts left ruts in the ground. A club, long since obsolete, was devised with a small iron head to play shots from such ruts. It was called a *rut iron*. If you have one, don't sell it at a garage sale—it's worth some serious coin.

Ryder Cup A biennial team match play competition between professional golfers representing the United States and Europe. Named for Samuel Ryder and first officially conducted in 1927, it was originally contested between the United States and Great Britain. The British team was expanded to include all of Europe in 1979, thereby greatly increasing the level of competition. The site alternates between a U.S. course and a European venue, and the format of play includes foursomes (alternate shot), four-ball (best ball), and singles matches (see *foursomes, four-ball, singles*).

S

saddleback A green that rises to a hump in the middle then drops off again toward the rear or sides (depending on which way the hump crosses the green) is known as a *saddleback* green.

sand The term *sand* refers to the sand in bunkers (see *bunker*). If you hit a shot in a sand bunker, you can just say, "I'm in the *sand*."

sandbagger A *sandbagger* is a player who purposely posts false or inflated scores in order to achieve a handicap higher than that which his ability war-rants. Another good way to refer to such a player is cheater.

sandblaster An alternate term for a sand wedge (see *sand wedge*). Don't use it.

sand iron An alternate term for a sand wedge. Use it only if you wish to sound like you've never before played the game.

sand save When you hit your ball into the sand and go on to make a par, that's a *sand save*. The *save* part refers to saving par when it appeared possible you might make a higher score.

sand shot Any shot played from the sand is a *sand shot*.

sand trap An alternate way of referring to any bunker with sand in it. Real golfers seldom use the term *sand trap*, opting instead for *bunker*.

sand wedge The *sand wedge* is a club designed specifically for playing short shots from the sand. The club typically has a loft of 56 degrees and a lie of 63 to 65 degrees. The club is designed with a rather large flange (see *flange*) that, after the clubhead has penetrated the sand, causes the club to deflect upward, preventing it from digging too far into the sand. The club was invented by Gene Sarazen, who claimed the idea for it came to him while flying in a plane with legendary tycoon Howard Hughes. (Sarazen said the way the plane reacted when Hughes moved the steering device started him thinking about a club for effectively playing from the sand.) The club is typically used for shots other than sand shots, however, due to its tremendous loft.

sandy When you get up and down (see *up and down*) from a bunker to save par, you've made a *sandy*. You should avoid this term unless you're playing in a betting match where *sandies* are part of the junk (see *junk*). Otherwise, it's wimpy sounding.

Sarazen, Gene One of the game's most historic figures, Gene Sarazen is one of only four men to win each of the major professional championships at least once during his career. His seven major championships began with the 1922 U.S. Open and ended with the 1935 Masters, during which he hit the most famous shot in golf history. Trailing Craig Wood by three shots in the final round, Sarazen holed

AP/WIDE WORLD PHOTOS

Gene Sarazen in 1932.

out a four-wood shot on the fifteenth hole for a double eagle—three under par on a single hole. He defeated Wood the following day in a playoff. Sarazen also invented the sand wedge (see *sand wedge*). A neat little side note in Sarazen's life is that as a kid he caddied at the Apawamis Club in New York with Ed Sullivan, who grew up to be a television host and even more famous than Sarazen. As of this writing, Sarazen, born in 1902, is still alive and living in Marco Island, Florida.

save par Any time you make a par when it appeared likely that you might make a higher score, you've *saved par*. Typically, you would say you saved par after getting up and down (see *up and down*) or after making a very long putt for par.

saw, big ol' If you hit a wild slice (see *slice*), you could jokingly describe it as a *big ol' saw*.

scare In old, old wooden clubheads, the *scare* was a notch or joint in the clubhead to which the shaft was attached. The scare predates wood clubheads made with sockets (see *socket*), which were introduced at the end of the 1800s. The term is borrowed from the Old Norse word *skor*, which was a joint in a ship's planking.

scare the hole A putt that appears destined to drop but just misses is said to *scare the hole*. Typically, this is used in a negative sense for a lousy putt, i.e., "I didn't even *scare the hole*."

scats A betting game typically played between three players, with each hole worth a fixed amount of money. If one of the three players wins the hole outright, he wins the predetermined amount of money from the other two players. If there is a tie for low ball, the value of the hole carries over (see *carryover*).

sclaff When your club bounces off the ground before striking the ball, it's cool to refer to it as a *sclaff*, or say, "I *sclaffed* it." (See *dropkick*.) The word is derived from the sound the club makes while bouncing off the ground.

score Your *score* for the hole is the total number of strokes (see *stroke*) played on that hole, and your *score* for a round is the total number of strokes played in a round.

scorecard The card on which a player records the scores for a round is called a *scorecard* (see *card*). The *scorecard* is also used to record handicaps and the progress of betting matches. The *scorecard* typically has hole yardages, hole handicap ratings, and local rules printed on it.

scoring clubs *Scoring clubs* refers to the iron clubs a player feels he can play accurately toward the hole, perhaps hitting the ball close enough that it will require only one putt to hole out. Typically, the scoring clubs would be considered the seven-iron through the wedges.

scoring lines The grooves on a club-face are sometimes referred to as *scoring lines,* although *scoring* refers to any notch or incision on the clubface, such as the dot scoring on some wedges. From the Old Norse word *skor.*

Scotch foursome A term originated by Americans to help clear up the confusion surrounding the terms *foursomes* and *four-ball* (see *foursomes* and *four-ball*). What confusion? In the United States, we refer to any group of four players as a foursome. In Great Britain, foursomes are matches where the partners alternate shots with a single ball (called alternate shot in the United States). In the United States, we never use the term *four-ball,* which is the British equivalent of our best-ball match. (*Four-ball* refers to the four balls in play.) The confusion arises every other year when the Ryder Cup

rolls around, since the Cup matches use the terms *foursome* and *four-ball* in the British sense. As a result, some American writers took to calling four-somes in the British sense *Scotch four-somes,* so their readers could distinguish between the British usage and the typical American usage of *foursome.*

scramble The term *scramble* has two uses. The first refers to the act of hitting inconsistent shots yet still managing to make respectable scores. So if you hit a bad tee shot and a bad second shot, you're *scrambling* to make par. In this sense, *scramble* means "a disorderly struggle, as for something prized" (*Webster's New World Dictionary*). A person who plays golf in this manner, frequently salvaging good scores from bad situations, is known as a *good scrambler.* While he is playing, he is *scrambling.*

The second use of *scramble* refers to a format of tournament play. In a *scramble tournament,* each of the four players on a team hits a tee shot. The group determines which ball is the best of the four, and each player plays the second shot from that spot. The team continues to play all its shots in this manner until holing out.

scrape it around When you don't hit the ball that well but you manage to make a respectable score for the day (for you), you might tell your buddies over a cold one that you *scraped it around.*

scratch Most golfers yearn for the day when they can describe themselves as *scratch* players, because it means they have a handicap of zero. If you ever wondered why a zero handicap is referred to as scratch, it's a reference to the days when footraces were started from a line scratched in the dirt. The slower runners were allowed to start ahead of the line (their handicap), while the fastest runners, who had no handicap, started at the scratch.

scruff When you *scruff* it, you hit a little more grass than you intended to while attempting to hit the ball.

scuff A *scuff* is pretty much any bad shot when you hit the ground before the ball.

second On a par-four or par-five hole, you can refer to your second shot simply as your *second*, i.e., "I played a four-iron second into the tenth green."

secondary rough Sometimes referred to as the first cut of rough, *secondary rough* is the rough just off the fairway in a championship setup, separating the fairway from the primary rough— the really deep spinach.

Senior PGA Tour The series of organized events for professional golfers over the age of fifty, conducted by the PGA Tour (see *PGA Tour*).

Don January, Senior PGA Tour player.

SAM GREENWOOD/PGA TOUR

set A term in swing lexicon, it refers to the position when the wrists are fully cocked, roughly halfway through the backswing. The wrists remain *set* until they are uncocked in the downswing. A player who sets very early in the swing achieves an *early set*. Also, the momentary pause at the top of your backswing (see *pause at the top*) is sometimes referred to as *setting the club*.

setting them up When you're improving your lies, you're *setting them up*—*them* being the balls in this case.

settle When you want your ball to stop rolling on the green, ask it (nicely) to *settle*.

set up *Set up* describes the act of assuming the setup position (see *setup position*). You would set up to the ball (two words), but the position you assumed would be the setup (one word).

setup position The address position (see *address*) is sometimes referred to as the *setup position*. The term is used to describe a player's position just prior to the start of the actual swing. In the lexicon of swing mechanics, the setup position is considered part of the swing even though the club hasn't started away from the ball. The basics of the *setup position* for a normal shot would be the clubface aimed at target and the feet, knees, hips, and shoulders aimed along a line parallel to the target line (see *target line*). The setup position would also include the grip,

ball position, and posture the player uses (see *grip, ball position, posture*).

seven-iron An iron club with an approximate loft of 38 to 40 degrees and a lie of 61 to 63 degrees.

shaft The long, cylindrical part of a golf club by which it is swung is called the *shaft*. Shafts were originally made from ash wood, then hickory wood, and then steel. Today, shafts are made from steel, graphite, or titanium (a specialty metal made from sand). The top end of the shaft is covered with a grip (see *grip*), and the bottom end is attached to the clubhead. Modern shafts are made with varying degrees of flex (see *flex*), which a player selects based on how fast he swings the club.

shag bag A bag in which a player keeps his own personal stash of practice balls is a *shag bag*. Practice shots are sometimes referred to as *shags*.

shallow A bunker is *shallow* if it has no lip or face of which to speak. Your swing is *shallow* if it is flat (see *flat*), which could be why you hit a lot of shots thin (see *thin*).

shank The *shank* is golf's version of a horror movie. You're aiming at a target, and your ball flies at a right angle to that target. What happened? The ball impacted with the hosel of the club (see *hosel*), which is not exactly the preferred way of contacting the ball. Where's the term come from? *Shank* is a term meaning "the part between the handle and the working part of a tool" (*Webster's New World Dictionary*). Even the worst of golfers know that the hosel is not the working part of their tool, the golf club.

shape a shot When you intentionally make the ball curve in flight, you're *shaping a shot.*

shoot There is only one use for this term. After a player has completed his round, you might ask, "What did you *shoot?*" What you want to know is his score for the round or a nine (see *nine*). If you want to immediately identify yourself as someone who knows absolutely nothing about the game, ask someone, "What kind of game do you *shoot?*" or "How do you *shoot?*" when you want to know what type of player they are. When they walk away from you without answering, you'll know why there's only one use for the term *shoot.* You don't shoot birdies, pars, or bogeys, and you don't shoot a score for a hole. The only thing you

can *shoot* is a total score for your round or a nine.

shooting the lights out When you are hitting every shot just right and making some low scores, you're *shooting the lights out.*

short When a putt stops before reaching the hole, it's *short.* When a shot intended to reach the green doesn't reach the green, it's *short.* When your swing doesn't reach parallel (see *parallel*) with the driver, it's *short.* If you're under five feet tall, you're short, but that's neither here nor there.

short course A *short course* can be a course made up of mostly shortish holes, with a total yardage that is not considered long enough to test the slightly-better-than-average golfer. There are a few older clubs in America that have a small course on the grounds in addition to the regular course. An example of this is the par-three course at Augusta National Golf Club. Sleepy Hollow Country Club in Scarborough, New York, also has a small course consisting of a few holes intended for practice or to sate the appetite of a golfer who has played a round and would like to play a few more holes. So, too, does Pine Valley

Golf Club in Clementon, New Jersey. Typically, such a course is referred to as a *short course*.

short game Collectively, the act of hitting pitches, chips, bunker shots, and putts is known as the *short game*, both because these shots travel only short distances and because they require short swings.

short grass When your tee shot lands on the fairway, it's on the *short grass*. Typically, you would use this to find the bright side of an otherwise lame drive that ends up in the fairway. "At least it's on the short grass," you might say.

short hole It is not uncommon to refer to a par three as a *short hole*— unless, of course, you have to hit your driver to reach the green.

short irons The iron clubs with which short approach shots are intended to be played are collectively called the *short irons*. There is no clear line of delineation between the mid-irons (see *mid-irons*) and the short irons, but you're safe calling the eight-iron on up your *short irons*.

shot A *shot* is any stroke (see *stroke*) recorded by actually striking the ball with a club. It doesn't matter which club you use; if you hit the ball, it's a *shot*. Also, when you are going to attempt to work the ball (see *work the ball*), you might say, "I'm going to hit a shot here."

shotgun start Some for-fun-only tournaments position groups on each tee of a course to start a round so all the participants can finish at roughly the same time. Such a beginning to a round is known as a *shotgun start* because back in the old days a gun would be fired to let the groups know it was okay to start (they could hear it no matter where they were on the course). Today, it is more common to ring a bell or blow a horn to signal the start of a *shotgun* event.

Shot Heard 'Round the World When Gene Sarazen (see *Sarazen, Gene*) holed out his second shot at the par-five fifteenth hole in the 1935 Masters, it was the *Shot Heard 'Round the World*. Sarazen beat Craig Wood in a playoff the next day.

shotmaker A player who is capable of creating a variety of ball flights— i.e., a low hook, a high fade, a knock-down shot (see *knockdown shot*)—and who can hit these shots as the circum-

STAN BADZ/PGA TOUR

Corey Pavin is a quintessential shotmaker.

stances of a round dictate is known as a *shotmaker*. Today, with the proliferation of game improvement clubs (see *game improvement clubs*), such players are rare, since these clubs lend themselves to hitting straight shots. It is not uncommon for traditionalists to lament the absence of shotmakers in the modern game, since *shotmaking* added an element of grace and style that is seldom seen anymore. Of the great modern players, Seve Ballesteros, Lee Trevino, and Corey Pavin are perhaps the best shotmakers.

shot pattern Your overall ball flight tendencies on a given day are your *shot patterns*.

shut Your club is considered *shut* at the top of your swing if the face of the club is in a position that, if it were at impact, would be closed (see *closed*) or aimed left of the target. When your club is shut at the top, the lead edge is almost vertical to the ground, as opposed to the roughly 45-degree angle to vertical which it should be.

side Each nine hole group of a golf course is called a *side*. You would use this in betting parlance to refer to the number of shots you were giving or getting per nine holes, for instance, "I'm getting two shots a side."

side bet A *side bet* is any bet made outside of and in addition to the main bet in a match. For example, if a Nassau bet (see *Nassau*) is being contested by two teams, the players may also opt to bet on the low individual medal (see *medal play*). Such a bet would be a side bet.

sidehill lie If you take your stance and the ball is above your feet or below your feet, you have a *sidehill lie*. When the ball is above your feet, the tendency is to hook it. When it's below your feet, the tendency is to slice it.

sidehiller A putt that breaks (see *break*) from right to left or from left to right is frequently referred to as a *sidehiller*, meaning the movement of the ball will be influenced by the side of a hill in the green.

sidesaddle A style of putting popularized by the great Sam Snead when he had putting woes, the *sidesaddle* method of putting places the player's chest and toes directly facing the line of putt (see *line of putt*) or the hole, as opposed to being parallel to the line of putt. Also, the club is gripped with the left hand on top of the shaft and the right hand far down the shaft. The stroke is basically a shove with the right hand, with the left hand acting as an anchor.

sign your card At the end of a tournament round, the players sign their cards to acknowledge that they did indeed shoot the score recorded on the card. It's an important thing since if you sign for an incorrect score that is lower than your actual score, you're disqualified from the event. Sign for a higher score, and that score stands, as Roberto DeVicenzo found out at the 1968 Masters when his scorecard

had one stroke too many on it. The score he signed for stood, and he missed out on a playoff with Bob Goalby by that one shot. Also, if you refuse or forget to sign your card, you're disqualified.

single caddie A *single caddie* is a club caddie who carries only one bag, typically due to the fact that he is not strong enough to carry two. When you carry one bag as a caddie, you are carrying *singles*.

singles In team match play competition, such as the Ryder Cup, when two players square off *mano a mano* in quest of a point for their team, they are playing a *singles* match. The term refers to a single player representing his team as opposed to a partnership doing the same.

singles hitter In baseball, a singles hitter is a player who does not hit for power but makes solid contact and places his hits with precision. So it is in golf—a *singles hitter* doesn't hit the ball great distances, but he does hit it with control.

sink When your intention is to make a putt, you are trying to *sink* it. When you do so, you've sunk it. Afterwards, you would say, "I sank a 76-foot putt at the ninth for birdie."

sit down When you hit a shot too hard, you want it to *sit down*. The key to using this phrase is proper volume. As your pitch shot is flying over the flagstick or your skulled chip shot (see *skull*) is dancing across the green, you should yell loudly, "Sit down!" which means you want the ball to stop dead in its tracks. It doesn't always work, but you might feel better after letting off some steam.

sitting up You're on the tee at the seventeenth hole in the final round of the U.S. Open. You're feeling the pressure and you hit a stinker. It's a wild slice headed directly for knee-high rough. You slouch off the tee, convinced you'll be lucky to find your ball, let alone be able to hit it. You arrive at your ball, and, lo and behold, it's not sitting deep down in the grass. Rather, it's perched atop the grass, and you can hit a normal shot. Your ball is *sitting up* in the rough.

six-iron An iron club with approximately 33 to 36 degrees of loft and 60 to 61 degrees of lie.

60-degree wedge An iron club with 60 degrees of loft that is used for hitting short, soft shots to the green.

skull When you contact the ball with the lead edge (see *lead edge*) in the cen-

ter of the ball, sending it lower and with more force than you intended, you've skulled it. Also, when former President Gerald Ford hit a spectator in the head with his ball, he *skulled* him.

sky When you pop the ball seemingly straight up into the air when you intended to hit it on a normal trajectory, you've *skied* it—sent it straight for the sky.

slam dunk A putt that is traveling much too fast to go into the hole but drops anyway is a *slam dunk*. To hole a *slam dunk*, the ball must either roll into the direct center of the hole or hit the back of the hole, pop up in the air, and fall in.

Sleepers A group of really scary sounding bunkers on the third hole at Prestwick in Scotland.

slice An out-of-control shot moving from left to right is a *slice*. Hit this type of shot frequently and you're a *slicer*.

slick If the greens are running fast (see *fast*), i.e., the ball moves quickly over the surface of the green with little force being applied to it, the greens are said to be slick.

slick slacks From the late 1960s to the mid-1980s, golfers unfortunately

AP/WIDE WORLD PHOTOS

Doug Sanders golfs in slick slacks in 1963.

loved to wear polyester trousers that did not require a belt. The polyester material, combined with typically garish colors, gave the pants a sheen that led to their christening as *slick slacks*. One of the great moments in the history of the game occurred when golfers ceased wearing slick slacks.

slide A putt that breaks subtly in either direction is said to *slide*. Also, if in the downswing your body moves laterally toward the target instead of turning toward the target, you *slide* toward the ball as opposed to turning through the ball. In this sense, an excessive slide is a no-no.

slider A putt that breaks just a tad in either direction is a *slider*. Also, a shot played with the intent of it moving from left to right and bouncing toward the hole once it's on the green is called a *slider*.

slip the club under the ball Any time you're playing a greenside shot that requires the club to pass underneath the ball and pop it into the air, your swing is an attempt to *slip the club under the ball* rather than hit the ball on the downswing.

slope system A handicap system that rates courses based on difficulty and assigns them a number so that the amount of handicap strokes given to a visiting player is based on how difficult the course is compared to the one he normally plays.

slow Greens are *slow* if the ball doesn't roll particularly fast on them. You're swing is *slow* if it is unhurried. And the pace of play (see *pace of play*) is *slow* if you have to wait to play every shot.

slump Just as in any other sport, if you're playing like a dog, you're in a *slump*.

smile When most golf balls had soft, balata covers, any shot hit with the lead edge of the club (see *lead edge*) produced a *smile* on the ball, i.e., a cut in the cover that resembled a person smiling.

smoked it When you hit a ball super far, you've *smoked it*, the idea being that you hit it so hard the friction between the club and ball started a fire.

smother hook A hooked shot (see *hook*) that flies low to the ground and not very far is a *smother hook*. The term refers to the fact that you smothered the ball with a severely closed (see *closed*) clubface.

snake An extremely long putt that breaks in multiple directions is known as a *snake*. If you need an explanation for why it's called a snake, you need to subscribe to *National Geographic*.

snap hook A shot that breaks off sharply to the left soon after being struck is a *snap hook*. It's the same as a duck hook (see *duck hook*).

Snead, Sam Perhaps the most naturally talented American-born player ever, Snead's longevity was amazing. He won seven major championships and finished third in the 1974 PGA Championship at the age of 61. Snead's swing was as fluid as that of

An intense Sam Snead, 1937.

AP/WIDE WORLD PHOTOS

anyone who ever played the game. He won each of the major championships at least once—except for the U.S. Open, in which he had several near misses and several disasters but never grabbed the brass ring.

sniper In the military sense, a sniper is a marksman who expertly conceals himself and shoots individual targets at will. In golf, a sharply hooked shot (see *duck hook* or *snap hook*) is called a *sniper* by golfers who know the language of the game. The allusion is that the ball was shot out of the air by a sniper. This shot is also known as a *snipe hook*.

snowman No one likes to admit it, but it happens. You make a score of eight for a given hole. That's a *snow-*

man, so named because the digit eight resembles a man of snow (see *Frosty*).

socket The socket is the part of the clubhead (see *clubhead*) into which the shaft is inserted.

soft ball A ball with a balata cover is often referred to as a *soft ball* because it feels softer than a two-piece ball (see *balata, two-piece ball, three-piece ball*).

sole The bottom of a clubhead—the part that generally comes in contact with the ground as you address the ball—is the *sole*. When you touch this part of the club on the ground as you address the ball, you are said to have *soled* the club.

sole plate Woods constructed of actual wood have metal *sole plates* screwed into their bottoms. This helps prevent erosion and covers up the drill holes that the clubhead acquires during construction.

solid ball The two-piece ball (see *two-piece ball*) is sometimes called a *solid ball* both because of its construction and feel.

spade When clubs had names, a six-iron was a *spade*.

Spanish Armada In Ryder Cup play, the Spanish partnership of Severiano

Ballesteros and Jose Maria Olazabal compiled an 11-2-3 record from 1987 through 1993. This invincible duo became known as the *Spanish Armada*—except they didn't sink like the historic Spanish Armada did.

Fellow countrymen and Ryder Cup partners Seve Ballesteros and Jose Maria Olazabal became known as the Spanish Armada.

Spectacles A pair of bunkers resting side-by-side that resemble a pair of eyeglasses at the fourteenth hole at Carnoustie (Scotland).

spike Each metal cleat on the bottoms of golf shoes is a *spike*. Also, some golfers refer to their shoes as a whole as *spikes*.

spiked up Greens with a lot of spike marks on them (see *spike marks*) are said to be *spiked up*.

spike marks The small pockmarks left on the green by golf shoe spikes are called *spike marks*. If a spike mark is in your line of putt, it's illegal to tamp it down, which makes for a great excuse for a missed putt—an excuse the pros often utilize.

split fairway A fairway that is actually divided into two separate avenues of approach to the green is a *split fairway*.

split the fairway A drive that flies directly down the center of the fairway is said to *split the fairway*, the implication being that the ball split the fairway into two even halves.

spin When you talk about *spin* on the ball, you're usually referring to backspin (see *backspin*).

spinach Slang for rough.

spin rate The rate at which a ball spins when hit.

spine angle The angle of a player's back at address is his *spine angle*.

splash Sometimes the technique for playing greenside sand shots is referred to as *splashing* the ball from the sand. Why? Because from a normal lie, a properly executed sand shot creates a halo of sand that looks like a small *splash* in water. And while we're on the subject of water, you might say you *splashed* one after you have hit a ball in the water.

spoon For a long time, *spoon* referred to a variety of wooden clubs. There were long spoons, short spoons, and so on. However, at some point in the first quarter of the twentieth century, *spoon* became synonymous with the three-wood.

spray When your shots fly every which way and you really don't have a clue where the next one might go, you're *spraying* them all over the place. Fore!

sprinkler head The irrigation systems on golf courses typically require *sprinkler heads* (the device that shoots water in various directions) to be scattered throughout the fairways and near greens. They make for a good excuse when your ball takes an unexpected bounce near the green. "Must have hit a sprinkler head," you might say while scratching your head.

square When the lead edge (see *lead edge*) of the club is pointed directly at the target at impact (see *impact*), you've achieved the ultimate goal of all golfers—a *square* clubface and a straight shot. Also, while you're taking your address position (see *address*), your body is *square* to the target line (see *target line*) if your feet, knees, hips, and shoulders are parallel to the target line. In the same position (address), the clubface is *square* if the lead edge is aimed directly at the target.

If you're playing in a match and the match is tied at any point, you might say your match is *square* or *all square*. It is not uncommon to hear television commentators refer to players tied for the lead as all square, but that's really not the proper usage for the term.

square grooves Grooves etched into the clubface in the shape of a U as opposed to the traditional V shape (see *box grooves*).

squeegee The things they push across the greens at professional tournaments to try to remove standing water on a rainy day.

squirt Any hideous, low sliced shot can be said to have *squirted* off the clubface.

Stableford scoring A system of scoring named for its inventor (Dr. Frank Stableford, Royal Liverpool Golf Club, 1931), *Stableford scoring* awards points to the player based on scores in relation to par. A bogey gets you one

point; a par, two points; a birdie, three points; an eagle, four points; and a double eagle, five points. Any score higher than bogey is zero points. It is common to modify this system to have high scores be negative points.

stadium golf A manner of golf course architecture pioneered by Pete Dye, *stadium golf* surrounds the holes with mounding that spectators can sit or stand on to get a clear view of the play (see *amphitheater*).

St. Andrews A town in Scotland recognized as the worldwide home of golf. The town is also home to the Old Course (see *Old Course*) and the Royal and Ancient Golf Club (see *Royal and Ancient Golf Club*).

starter The guy who tells you it's okay to tee off on the first hole is the *starter.*

starting time The time when your round is scheduled to begin.

stake it When you hit one really close to the hole with a full shot, you've *staked it*, or hit it close to the stake (the flagstick).

stance This term refers primarily to your feet as you set up to play a shot. When you are setting your feet in place, you are taking your *stance*. Your stance is open if your left foot is drawn back farther from the ball than your right foot, and it's closed if your left foot is closer to the ball than your right foot. The distance between your feet is your *stance width*.

stand on it When you assess a shot and decide you must hit a given club the absolute maximum distance that club can produce, you might say, "I've got to *stand on it* to get it there." In this case, *there* means the vicinity of the hole.

stay behind it A swing term that refers to the idea of avoiding lateral body movement through the ball.

steel shaft In the 1940s, *steel shafts* began to replace hickory wood as the predominant shaft type (see *shaft*). Byron Nelson is generally regarded as the first great player to make the switch to steel shafts.

steer An overly tense swing is sometimes referred to as an attempt to *steer the ball*, the allusion being that the player is afraid to relax and let the club do the work.

Stephenson, Jan A noteworthy competitor in women's golf, Stephenson initially gained fame because she was the sexiest woman golfer in the his-

Jan Stephenson in 1988.

AP/WIDE WORLD PHOTOS

tory of the professional game, an image she did not seem to mind. She could also play, winning three major women's championships including the 1982 LPGA Championship and the 1983 U.S. Women's Open.

stick *Stick* is short for the flagstick and, in turn, is a term used to describe the flagstick, the hole, and the area immediately surrounding the hole. If you intend to play a shot directly for the hole, you might say, "I'm going to fire right at the *stick*." Also, *stick* can be used to describe a shot that hits the green and stops immediately. It's not uncommon to hear a television commentator say, "Watch this stick," as a ball descends toward the green. Also, a player might say, "I'm going to *stick* it right in there," meaning he intends to get the subsequent shot very close to the hole.

Also, your golf clubs are your *sticks*. To ask someone what club they hit for a certain shot, say, "What stick did you use?" Also, you might say of a good player, "He's mean with the *stick*," or "He can give it some *stick*."

stiff When you hit a shot very close to the hole, you *stiffed it* or hit it *stiff*. Also, a shaft (see *shaft*) that bends very little while being swung is said to be *stiff*.

There are two slang uses for this term. A player who does not play well under pressure is a *stiff*, and a caddie who gets a lousy tip would say, "I got *stiffed*," typically while he's stealing balls out of the tightwad's bag to make up for the lack of proper compensation.

stimpmeter A *stimpmeter* is a little hand-held ramp used to determine the overall speed of the greens on a golf course. The person doing the measuring holds the stimpmeter at an angle, rolls balls down the ramp, and measures how far they go. Greens are measured in this way so that each green on a course is a consistent speed, particularly in preparation for tournament play. The speeds are recorded using numbers that relate to how far the ball went on the green after rolling down the ramp. Championship greens are typically in the area of between ten and twelve on the *stimpmeter*. The players would say the greens are *stimping* or *stimping* out at ten, for example. The typical golf course's greens might measure between seven and nine on the *stimpmeter*.

stipulated round In tournament play, you have to play the *stipulated round* in order for your score to count. This simply means you must play all 18 holes in the order they are supposed to be played.

stone dead Hit a shot close to the hole and you've hit it *stone dead*. To sound like a real golfer, say, "I hit it *stoney*." Just make sure you make the putt, or your pals will say you putt like Fred Flintstone.

stop One of the many ways to plead with your ball to stop its forward progress. The word must be used with a tone of despair. "*Stop!*"

stop the bleeding When your game is coming apart at the seams—for example, you're making bogey after bogey—a good hole or two in succession *stops the bleeding*. That is to say, you've temporarily halted your poor play.

straight-faced A club with comparatively little loft is sometimes described as *straight-faced*. Golf publications love to refer to the long irons as the "dangerously *straight-faced* long irons," a reference to the relative difficulty of hitting them properly.

straight left arm Considered a basic fundamental of a proper golf swing, a *straight left arm* refers to that arm staying straight most of the way through the backswing.

strategic A *strategic* course design is meant to challenge the player's thinking capacity as opposed to merely punishing poor shots (see *penal*). The strategic design requires the excellent player to determine the best approach to playing a hole rather than simply avoiding trouble, a mind-set one takes when playing a penal design.

striped it You might say of a well-hit tee shot, "I *striped it*." What does it mean? Your guess is as good as the author's.

striper A golf ball designated for practice purposes typically has a red stripe painted around it. This helps identify the ball for the person gathering them up. Such a ball is often referred to as a *striper*. If you want to suffer the maximum abuse possible for a golfer, tee up a striper during a round. Not only will you be immediately identified as a pathetic loser and thief, but the whole world will know you're cheap, too.

stroke The forward movement of the clubhead with the intent to hit the ball. If you stop before you hit the ball, you're okay—it doesn't count. Also, penalties are assessed in *strokes*, which means your total score isn't necessarily a reference to the number of times you hit the ball during the round.

stroke and distance If you hit your ball out-of-bounds, it's a two-stroke penalty, one stroke for the actual shot and one stroke to penalize you for the distance from where the ball landed back to its original point, which is where you must play from.

stroke play There are two standard methods of competition in golf. The original form was match play (see *match play*). The other form, prevalent in professional tournament competition, is *stroke play*, which determines a winner by totaling the number of strokes for one or more rounds.

strong grip If your right hand is turned underneath the shaft when you grip the club, you have a *strong grip*.

Paul Azinger uses a strong grip.

AP/WIDE WORLD PHOTOS

stymie The *stymie*, which was abolished in 1951, described a situation in match play wherein one player's ball blocked another's path to the hole. The only remedy for the player whose path was blocked (*stymied*) was to play around or over the intruding ball. The term is a bit confusing, however, because a ball played with the intention of blocking the hole was a stymie, as was any shot played in attempt to go around or over the ball.

The term is still used today, albeit infrequently, to describe any situation where a player feels his direct approach to his target is blocked by something such as a tree.

suck back A ball that hits a green and then reverses its direction is sometimes said to *suck back*. Many golfers seem to derive extreme delight from requesting this of their ball ("*Suck back!*"), but propriety prevents us from exploring the reasons for this.

sucker pin A *sucker pin* is any hole location cut close to or hidden behind a hazard such as a bunker or water hazard. The meaning of this term is clear. A smart player will not attempt to hit his ball directly at such a hole location. A *sucker* will and will likely pay the price of doing so in the currency of strokes.

sudden death When a match or tournament ends in a tie between two or more players, the most common method of breaking the tie is to proceed directly to extra holes and compete at *sudden death*, wherein the first player to win a hole outright wins the match or tournament. This manner of playoff, prevalent in nearly all professional golf championships save for the U.S. and British Opens, is the favorite of golf fans because it quickly determines a winner.

Sunday bag A *Sunday bag* is a small canvas golf bag without much support to it. The bags were popular in the days when golfers preferred to walk the golf course, particularly if they didn't employ a caddie. A Sunday bag is, in effect, little more than a sack with a thin strap attached to it.

Sunday pin placement Many tournament courses cut the hole in the same position for the final round year after year, typically in a spot that will create maximum excitement. Since the final round of most tournaments is played on Sunday, these hole placements became known as *Sunday pin placements.*

superintendent The modern green-keeper (see *greenkeeper*) often prefers to be called a *greens superintendent.* It's golf's version of a politically correct euphemism.

supination A mucked up way of saying your left arm turns counterclockwise through impact so that the palm eventually faces the sky in the follow through. If you're worried about *supination*, you probably can't hit the ball out of your own shadow.

surlyn The majority of golf balls made today are of the two-piece variety (see *two-piece ball*) and are covered with *surlyn*, a synthetic material that is difficult to cut, scrape, or otherwise damage without the use of an explosive device.

swale Gently rolling depressions in fairways or greens are often referred to as *swales.*

sway If you move your body laterally to the right on the backswing, rather than turning back as is deemed technically sound, you have a *sway* in your swing.

sweep The action of picking the ball off the ground with a fairway wood (see *pick it*), thereby avoiding solid contact with the ground, is known as *sweeping the ball.*

sweet If someone tells you one of your shots was *sweet*, say, "Thanks." Just like in any other phase of your life, something said to be sweet is generally perceived as something good.

sweet spot The spot on the clubface that, when contacted by the ball, produces the best possible result is the *sweet spot.* You'll know it when you feel it, partner, because the feeling runs right down to your toes and up your spine and makes your hair stand on end.

Swilcan Burn A tiny stream that fronts the first green at the Old Course (see *Old Course*). When the hole is cut in the front of the green, it's not uncommon for players to hit their balls in the Swilcan Burn, or for balls to hit the green and spin back into the water.

swing Gyrating, supinating, pronating, cocking, uncocking, shifting, turning, squaring—all that stuff you do in an attempt to hit the ball is, collectively, your *swing*. It may not be pretty, but it's all you've got. Someone attempting to describe the manner in which you swing would describe you as a fast (or slow or wild or controlled) *swinger*.

swing arc The path of the clubhead as it travels through the swing is the *swing arc*.

swing doctor Slang for teaching professional (see *teaching professional*), a profession that exists entirely due to the perplexing nature of the game.

David Leadbetter (crouching) is the best-known swing doctor.

swing key A single thought a player focuses on during his swing is a *swing key* (see *low and slow*).

swing path The path of the shaft of the club as it is swung.

swing plane *Swing plane* refers to the basic angle at which you keep the shaft throughout your swing.

swingweight The overall weight of a club is spoken of in terms of *swingweight*, a correlative measurement of the weight of the shaft and the clubhead.

swipe An out-of-control swing is sometimes referred to as a *swipe*.

S-word What's the dirtiest word in golf? The answer is *shank* (see *shank*), a shot that flies perpendicular to the target line after contacting the hosel (see *hosel*) of the club. So ugly and so contagious are shanks, some golfers cannot bring themselves to mutter the word for fear that they will be stricken with the affliction. When mentioning the word is unavoidable, those who live in fear call it the *S-word*. Does it work? Who knows, but at least it prevents the need to pronounce the nasty hard k at the end of the word, which some shankologists believe to be the cause of the dreaded shank.

T

tail on it, a little A sliced shot is sometimes said to have *a little tail on it*, which typically means it's only a moderate slice. Don't refer to a hook as having a tail on it. It just isn't done.

take a ball out of play When the cover of your ball is damaged, you can *take it out of play*, i.e., replace it with another one without penalty.

takeaway The initial phase of the backswing, beginning when the club starts back from the ball and ending when it begins to move upward, is known as the *takeaway*. The term refers to the idea of taking the club away from the ball.

take it away This is what you say to someone when you want to give them a putt (see *give a putt*). To note your concession, you'd simply say, "*Take it away.*"

take it back When you begin your backswing, you're *taking it back.*

take the pipe As if there weren't enough ways to describe the act of playing poorly under pressure, here's another one. When you *take the pipe,* it means you choked, pal. It's a reference to the act of inhaling fumes from a gas pipe or the tail pipe on a car.

talk to the ball Golfers are constantly searching for help and seem to be under the delusion that *talking to the ball* (or yelling at it) will someone have an impact on the shot in progress. That's why we say things such as, "Bite!" and "Sit down!" and "Chew!" Does the ball listen? It can't hurt.

tamp down a spike mark It's illegal to do it when a spike mark is in your line of putt (see *line of putt*), but you might *tamp down a spike mark* with the sole of your putter afterward as a courtesy to those playing behind you. By the way, to sound like a real golfer, you'll want to say tamp (which means to repeatedly pound something), as opposed to tap, because no one ever pushes down on a spike mark just once.

tap-in When your ball is so close to the hole that you can simply tap the ball into the hole without thinking about it, the putt is called a *tap-in*. Of course, golfers have a tendency to falsely identify putts as tap-ins, since an awful lot of them are tapped but don't go in. In any case, both the putt and the act of stroking it are known as *tap-ins*.

target golf When the fairways and greens of a course are virtual islands of turf surrounded by desert or unkempt landscape, as opposed to the course being unencumbered stretches of grass (except for hazards), the style of golf played is known as *target golf*.

target line An imaginary line extending from your ball to your target, whatever it happens to be.

teaching professional A golf professional who derives his income primarily from giving lessons to golfers is a *teaching professional*.

tee The modern *tee* is a small wooden peg used to prop up the ball for shots played from the tee box on a given hole. Some super geeks might use tees made of plastic, but a real golfer uses only wooden tees. In the game's formative years, players (or their caddies) would build small piles of sand, upon which they would place their balls. These little piles of sand were the first tees.

tee box In modern parlance, the *tee box* refers to the teeing area in general. When sand was used to make tees, a box containing sand was placed near the teeing area and called a *tee box*.

202

teed or **teed up** Once a ball is placed on a tee, it is said to be *teed* or *teed up*.

teeing ground The proper way of referring to the area from which play begins on each hole. You don't have to sound so proper, however. Just call it the tee.

tee it up When you want to know if your buddy wants to play golf, ask him if he wants to *tee it up*. You'll sound just like a real golfer, even if you don't play like one.

tee marker On each set of tees, there are two markers on the ground, spaced apart and perpendicular to the hole. They are the *tee markers*, and you must tee off between them and no more than two club lengths behind them.

tee off When you play a shot from the tee, you have *teed off*. You won't hear many real golfers use this except to refer to the time at which their round will begin, i.e., "What time do we *tee off?*" means what time will the tee shots be struck on the first hole.

tee shot A shot played from the teeing ground is your *tee shot*. On par fours and par fives, you can substitute the word *drive* for *tee shot*, but don't do so on a par three. On par threes, you definitely want to say tee shot.

tee-to-green The part of the game that involves playing full shots is known as the *tee-to-green* phase of the game.

tempo One of the most misunderstood words in the game, *tempo* refers to the idea of moving your body at roughly the same speed throughout your swing. The club picks up speed, but the body moves at the same speed throughout the swing. Most golfers think *tempo* means to swing slow, but that's not the case. However, the word's misused meaning is a good way of remembering to try to swing at a consistent pace.

temporary green When weather or maintenance dictate that the usual greens on a course be declared off-limits for play, courses set up *temporary greens* that are little more than holes cut in the fairway.

test Golf courses, particularly good ones, are often referred to as tests. A difficult course might be referred to as a solid, stern, difficult, or demanding *test* or *test of golf*.

tester A putt that's too long to be a tap-in (see *tap-in*) but short enough that a good player should make it, is sometimes called a *tester* because it will test his skill and nerve as a putter.

Texas wedge Any time you use your putter from off the green, it's referred to as a *Texas wedge*, especially if you use it from the fairway. The shot was popularized in Texas, where the firm ground and high winds sometimes made it easier to play the ball along the ground with the putter rather than risk the wind affecting the ball or the clubhead bouncing off the hardpan and skulling the ball (see *hardpan* and *skull*).

thin When the lead edge (see *lead edge*) of the clubhead contacts the ball rather than sliding underneath it, the shot is said to be hit *thin*. There are different levels of thin shots, based primarily on where the lead edge contacts the ball. When the lead edge contacts the ball below the center of the ball, the shot is usually not too bad. If contact occurs in the center of the ball or above, you've got problems.

thin to win This expression refers to the idea that if you're going to mis-hit a shot by hitting it either fat (see *fat*) or thin, you'll almost always get a better result by hitting it thin because a slightly thin shot has some redeeming qualities, such as distance and spin. A fat shot just stinks.

three-ball match Suppose you and two of your buddies can't find a fourth person to round out your group, but you'd still like to play a match. In a *three-ball match*, each player plays an individual match against the other two, i.e., you play two singles matches at the same time.

three-iron An iron club with approximately 23 to 25 degrees of loft and approximately 57 to 59 degrees of lie.

three-jack Slang expression for three putts on a single green.

three-piece ball The three parts of a *three-piece ball* are a rubber core, a thick layer of thin rubber bands, and the cover. Such a ball is also frequently called a wound ball, a reference to the tightly wound rubber bands.

three-putt If you're looking to run up your score in a hurry, mix in a few *three-putts*. The term refers to any green on which you take three putts to hole out.

three-quarter shot When you play a shot with a swing three-quarters of the length typical for playing a full shot with the chosen club, you've played a *three-quarter shot*. You might play such a shot when the full value of the club would produce too long of a shot.

three-shotter A par-five hole that requires even the longest hitters to play three shots to get to the green is called a *three-shotter*.

threesome Any group made up of three players is called a *threesome*. There is also a type of match called a *threesome* in which a single player competes against two partners who play alternate shots.

three-wood A wood club with approximately 15 to 17 degrees of loft and 55 to 57 degrees of lie.

through the green See *green, through the*.

throw-up zone A putt short enough that an expert player should make it but long enough to test his nerves is said to be in the *throw-up zone*, meaning a nervous person might vomit while pondering the situation.

tiered green Any green with distinct vertical levels is known as a *tiered green*. The individual levels are known as tiers.

tiger country Heavy, heavy rough is sometimes called *tiger country*, a reference to the fact that deep rough is sometimes called jungle (see *jungle*).

tiger tees An alternate way of referring to the championship tees (see *championship tees*), *tiger tees* allude to the idea that you'd have to be a real tiger to handle a course from the back tees. Frankly, you'd sound like a real sissy using this term. (Also see *pro tees*.)

tight A hole is said to be *tight* if it has a narrow driving area closely lined by trees, bunkers, or out-of-bounds. If most of the holes on a golf course fit this description, the entire course is described as *tight*.

Also, if your ball is sitting on very little grass, with very little cushion between the ball and the soil, the lie is described as a *tight* lie. Sometimes, if the grass is cut exceedingly short, you might even have a tight lie in the fairway.

A shot that stops very close to the hole is sometimes described as being *tight* to the hole. If you hit a shot that you think is heading for the vicinity of the hole, you might decide to yell, "Get tight!" in the hopes that your ball is listening.

If a player appears to be tense, or his swing displays obvious signs of tension, he is sometimes referred to as being *tight*.

Finally, if a caddie thinks the person he is caddying for is a cheapskate and very likely a poor tipper, he would describe the player as being *tight*, meaning he keeps a tight hold on his wallet and his cash.

timing As with many things involving the golf swing, the term *timing* is often misunderstood. Many golfers think it refers to the speed of the swing, but, in fact, it refers to the various elements of the swing happening in the proper sequence. In other words, if a player were to begin his downswing with his arms as opposed to his lower body (the opposite of the proper sequence), you would say he had poor *timing* because the sequence of motions in his swing was out of whack. On the other hand, some players have unusual movements in their swings but are nevertheless fine ballstrikers (see *ballstriking*). In such a case, it is almost inevitable that superb timing is the reason the player hits the ball solidly. That is to say, despite the fact he makes some funky moves, he makes them in the proper sequence to ensure solid contact.

tin cup Most cup liners (see *cup liner*) are made of plastic these days, but there was a time when many were made of tin. Such a cup liner was referred to as a *tin cup* and was easy to notice since the ball made a clanking sound when it hit the bottom of the cup.

tips The tees from which a course plays longest are sometimes referred to as the *tips*.

tired swing It is not uncommon for a player to grow physically or mentally weary toward the end of a round, particularly after several consecutive days of tournament play. Such fatigue often brings about *tired swings*, which is a way of saying the player has lost his tempo or timing and, as a result, is hitting shots uncharacteristic of the level of play that preceded the tired swings.

titanium A specialty, lightweight metal made from sand and used to construct some shafts and clubheads.

toe The end of the clubhead, particularly the point on the clubface farthest from the shaft, is known as the *toe* of the club.

toed in Some specialty shots, such as a punch hook (see *punch shot*) require the player to toe the club in at address. This means that the toe of the club is closer to the ball than the heel of the club, or it is *toed in.* When the club is *toed in,* the lead edge is aimed left of the target, and the ball will curve from right to left if properly struck.

toe job When you hit one way out on the toe of the club (see *toe*), you can explain the weak shot by saying you hit a *toe job.* Typically, the ball will hook as a result of a toe job.

took a look in the hole A ball that rolls closely by the hole but doesn't fall in *took a look in the hole.*

took your eye off it When you top a shot (see *top*), somebody will tell you that you *took your eye off it.* Just tell them to shut up.

too much When you hit a putt too hard to go in the hole or hit a club and send a shot flying over the green, you might say, "That's *too much,*" meaning either the putt was played with too much force or the full shot was played with too much club, too much force, or both.

top When the lead edge (see *lead edge*) of the club contacts the upper one-third of the ball, you've *topped it.* When you *top it,* the ball simply dribbles along the ground for the majority of its forward progress. Such a shot

can be caused by a wide range of mishaps in the swing.

top line When you address the ball and look down at the club, the top part of an iron club is the *top line.*

top of his game A player who is playing as well as he is capable of playing, both in terms of hitting the ball and his mental approach, is said to be at the *top of his game.*

top of the swing When the club ceases moving back and up, you've

ARCHIVES/PGA TOUR

Tom Lehman is pictured at the top of his swing.

reached the *top of your swing.* (Also see *pause at the top.*)

topspin When the ball is spinning forward, or toward the target, it has *topspin* on it. For the most part, the ball has to contact the ground for *topspin* to be created. Even on a putt, the ball skids along the ground initially before it begins spinning forward. And, despite the fact that a full shot may bounce forward after hitting the ground, it does so as the result of the ball ricocheting off the ground, not because of topspin created by the club.

torque *Torque* is the twisting of the shaft and the clubhead as a result of impact with the ball. Other than at impact, the shaft of your club doesn't torque. It may bend, but it doesn't twist.

torture chamber A very difficult golf course, especially if it has an abundance of hazards, is sometimes referred to as a *torture chamber.* Also, even if the course is easy but you play poorly, you might say, "Man, it was like a *torture chamber* out there today."

toss balls So you and your three pals are standing around on the first tee, waiting to get the round started. You want to have a little bet, but you're not sure how to pick the partners. Why not leave it to chance, you decide. So you *toss balls* to decide on partners. That is, each player gives one ball to the person who will *toss* them into the air. The two balls sitting closest to each other after the balls come to rest on the ground are partners, as are the remaining two balls.

touch The ability to play delicate shots from off the green that come to rest near the hole is known as *touch.* Such a shot is known as a *touch shot.* Also, a player who is a good putter is often said to have a great *touch* on the greens.

touch of class This is what you might say to someone after they execute a shot requiring a deft touch (see *touch*).

tour A series of organized events, typically arranged so that professional golfers can compete for prize money, is known as a *tour.* The word is usually preceded by the name of the organizing association, i.e., the PGA Tour (see *PGA Tour*). There are many other tours in addition to the top-level tours, however, such as minitours (see *minitour*) and junior tours (in which junior golfers compete as amateurs). However, when you refer to *the tour*, you're talking about the PGA Tour. If you mean to refer to the Senior Tour or the LPGA Tour, you must use the full expression because the PGA Tour is the only *the tour* out there. *The tour* is also an acceptable way to refer to the corporate organization (also known as the PGA Tour) that conducts the PGA Tour.

tour blade With the advent and rise in popularity of perimeter-weighted clubs (see *perimeter-weighted clubs*), the use of forged irons (see *forged iron*) became almost strictly the domain professional tour players. Many, but not all, tour players prefer forged irons because of the feel (see *feel*) of shots struck with them and for the feedback they provide. As a result of this, forged irons are commonly referred to as *tour blades, blade* referring to the thin top line and small clubhead of forged clubs (see *top line*).

tour caddie A person who makes his living caddying for professional tour players is a *tour caddie*.

tour card A player who meets certain qualifying standards (different for each professional tour), which permit play in professional tour events for an entire year, is said to have his *tour card* or, simply, his *card*. If at the end of that year the player does not once again

meet the qualifying standards and is forced to give up his card, he is said to have lost his card.

tour event Each of the individual tournaments making up a professional tour is known as a *tour event*.

tournament A *tournament* is any event in which players, playing individually or as teams, compete versus the rest of the field of players to become the sole winner of the event, be it match play or stroke play, professional or amateur, one round or more.

tournament committee The *tournament committee* is the group of people who organize the details and interpret the Rules of Golf for a tournament at the club level. At the professional level, the *tournament committee,* typically made up of members from the host club, handles the logistics that the conducting organization does not handle. At the professional level, however, the rules are left to the experts.

tournament tough A player who has played in, and done well in, a lot of tournaments is often referred to as *tournament tough*, a reference to the fact that he should be mentally capable of handling the pressure of tournament golf.

tourney An alternate word for *tournament*.

tour player A person who plays on an organized professional tour on a regular basis is known as a *tour player*.

tour stop Events scheduled on a professional tour are sometimes referred to as *tour stops*, i.e., the tour has stopped for the week in a given city.

tour van Some equipment manufacturers have mobile equipment repair shops that follow the professional tours from town to town. Such a vehicle is known as a *tour van*.

TPC These three initials in the name of a golf course stand for Tournament Players Club and indicate that the course was built in conjunction with the PGA Tour. There was a time when the corporate part of the PGA Tour saw potential in the owning and operating of golf courses, particularly ones that could be promoted as being the site of a PGA Tour event. Most *TPC* courses are built as stadium courses (see *stadium golf*), which allows for superb viewing of tournament play.

TPC at Sawgrass, Stadium Course Home of the Players Championship on the PGA Tour, the Stadium Course at the TPC at Sawgrass was the first of its type (designed by Pete Dye) and ushered in the modern era of architecture. Its most famous hole is the 132-yard seventeenth, with its oft-photographed island green.

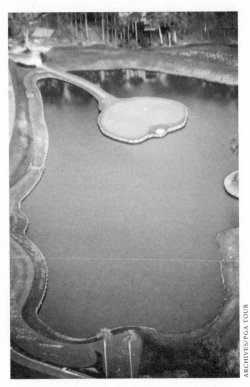

TPC Sawgrass's seventeenth boasts a treacherous island green.

track In its most common form, *track* is slang for a golf course. Typically, the term is used to describe a course as a good *track*, meaning a fine course. A dog track is a lousy course.

Also, sometimes a putt is said to *track* toward the hole, which means it follows a perfect line from the moment it leaves the clubface until it goes directly into the center of the hole, never leaving a question that it will do anything but go in the hole. A putt that does so is said to be *tracking*.

track iron An alternate term for a rut iron (see *rut iron*), named for the tracks left by wagon wheels as they moved across a golf course.

transition The *transition* part of the golf swing refers to the moment when the backswing changes into the downswing. The *transition* begins just prior to the instant the club reaches the point farthest from the ball, the moment when the hips begin to turn toward the target while the club finishes moving back. (See *pause at the top*.)

transition area A *transition area* is a large sandy area on a golf course that, for reasons of saving money on maintenance, is left uncovered with grass. A *transition area* is not a hazard and can usually be identified by the fact that it has no discernible lip. Most transition areas are typically identified as such on the scorecard.

trap An alternate word for a bunker, *trap* is a word that you should avoid using if you want to sound like a real golfer.

Trevino, Lee A six-time major championship winner, Trevino is perhaps the premier shotmaker of all time (see *shotmaker*). His Mexican heritage makes him unique among the game's great players. He is also well-known for his biting wit and happy-go-lucky demeanor when he is playing well. When he's not playing well, he's not quite so happy-go-lucky. Nicknamed the Merry Mex, Trevino was a fierce competitor in his heyday, winning two U.S. Opens in four years (1968 and 1971).

Lee Trevino

triangle The *triangle* in your swing refers to the angle of your two arms as you address the ball. The idea is to keep the triangle they form (along with your chest) intact as you start the club away from the ball.

triple bogey A score of three-over par on a given hole is a *triple bogey*. To sound like a real golfer, you would simply refer to it as a *triple*.

trolley An Anglicism for a pull cart (see *pull cart*). Ask for a *trolley* at a U.S. course, and they'll tell you to try a street corner in San Francisco.

trouble Anytime your ball ends up in a place you'd rather it hadn't—in a bunker, in a hazard, in the bushes—you've found *trouble*. Find it too often, and you might want to find a new game.

trouble shot A shot played to escape from trouble is known as a *trouble shot*.

trust it Professional golfers, despite their long hours of practice, still encounter moments of self-doubt, just like all golfers. At such moments, a tour player's caddie will sometimes say to the player just prior to a shot, "*Trust it*." What does it mean? It means to trust that the swing the player is about to make will be a good one and produce a good shot.

turn As it relates to your swing, *turn* refers to the rotation of your body away from and through the ball.

turn, the When a player finishes the ninth hole and is making his way toward the tenth tee, he has made *the turn* from the front nine to the back nine (see *front nine* and *back nine*). A player's score for the first nine holes is said to be his score *at the turn*, e.g., "I was two under *at the turn*."

turn it over When a player says he wants to *turn it over*, it means he wants to make the ball curve from right to left. You can turn it over only from right to left. You'd never use this term to describe the movement of the ball from left to right. Instead, you'd say you wanted the ball to slide (see *slider*).

twitch In the United States when a player gets a case of nerves on short putts, frequently missing them, it is known as the yips (see *yips*). The British refer to this affliction as *the twitch*. And as every golfer knows, once you've had 'em, you got 'em.

two-iron An iron with approximately 20 to 22 degrees of loft and approximately 57 to 59 degrees of lie.

two-piece ball A ball that consists only of a rubber core and a cover is a *two-piece ball*. Most golf balls manufactured and played today are of *two-piece* construction. Sometimes, a *two-piece ball* is referred to as a solid ball.

two-point match See *high-low*.

two-putt When you hole out on your second putt on a given hole, you have two-putted. The *two-putt* is considered regulation performance (see *regulation*) on a hole.

two-shotter Any hole that would typically require an expert player to play two shots to reach the green can be referred to as a *two-shotter*. This would include most par fours.

twosome A playing group consisting of two players is known as a *twosome*.

two-wood A wooden club with approximately 13 to 14 degrees of loft and 54 to 56 degrees of lie. Sometimes referred to as a brassie.

U

U and E shot Sometimes it's known as getting away with one. You hit a poor shot, but it turns out okay. Maybe you hit a low drive that isn't going to win a beauty contest, but it still gets you out in the fairway. That is to say, it's ugly but effective—a *U and E shot*.

ugly Even the language of golf isn't colorful enough to come up with a more concise way than this of describing a bad shot. When you hit a bad shot, it's *ugly*.

U-groove A groove etched into a clubface in the shape of a U (see *box grooves*).

uncock Your wrists should cock (see *cock*) early in your backswing and stay that way almost until the point that your arms return to the front of your body. At this point, the weight of the clubhead begins to *uncock*, or straighten, your wrists in preparation for impact. It's not a conscious move—in a good swing, it just happens.

underclub Any time a shot comes up short of your intended target solely because you didn't hit the proper club for the distance, you have *underclubbed*. Underclubbing is perhaps one of the five most common errors made by the average golfer.

under it, got When you pop a shot straight into the air, it's common to say, "I *got under it*." Whether or not you actually did get under the ball is another matter. This expression refers to the idea that you hit the shot high because you passed the clubhead too far under the ball. In reality, you probably hit down on the ball at too steep an angle.

under par When your running score for a round or your aggregate score for a tournament totals up to less than par, you are *under par*. To sound like a real golfer, you'd simply say *under* and drop the *par*. You'll be dropping a lot of putts, too—if you're under, that is.

underspin An old-fashioned way of referring to backspin, *underspin* is a good one to use to sound like you know something no one else does.

unload In the backswing, when the shaft flexes it is said to be loading or storing energy. When the energy is released in the downswing, the shaft has *unloaded*, creating some of the power that propels the ball.

unplayable lie You can decide that your ball is unplayable any time (except for when it's in a water hazard), but since it costs you a penalty stroke, you probably should save it for those times when you just can't get the club on the ball. Keep in mind that only you can declare your ball unplayable. When you do so, you have three options. You can drop it where you played the prior shot, move it two club lengths from the *unplayable lie*, or move it back as far as you want (unless you're in a bunker) on a straight line, keeping the unplayable point between you and the hole.

up When you hit a putt, it is *up* if it reaches a point level with the hole. You also might yell for a shot to get *up*, meaning you think it might end up short of your target. Also, if you're leading in match-play, you're *up* by however many holes you lead by. If you're ahead by three holes, you're three up.

up and down When you fail to hit a green in regulation (see *green in regulation*), your primary concern becomes getting *up and down*. This phrase refers to getting your next shot up (on the green) and the subsequent putt *down* (into the hole) to save par. More often than not, this refers to getting *up and down* from a greenside bunker, but it's also acceptable to use the phrase any time a player plays an excellent shot from elsewhere around the green and holes the putt.

uphill lie When your ball is sitting on terrain that leans directly away from the target, you have an *uphill lie*. The tendency is to pull the ball (see *pull*) from an uphill lie, so aim a little right.

upright Both your swing and your golf clubs can be *upright*. Your swing is *upright* if, in the backswing, the clubhead swings in a more vertical manner than would be considered on plane. Jack Nicklaus is the most famous player to have an *upright* swing. Also, if the lie of your clubs (see *lie*) is more vertical than that which is considered standard, your clubs are said to be *upright*.

upshoot An *upshoot* is a shot that comes off the clubface with a slightly higher trajectory than anticipated and which, as a result, flies a shorter distance than anticipated.

upswing Once every so often—about as often as Haley's Comet appears—someone decides to refer to the backswing as the *upswing*.

utility wood Any wood designed to play shots from difficult lies, such as from the rough. The design of *utility woods* is such that a player can use a wood in situations that previously required the use of an iron because the wood clubhead could not move through the grass.

United States Golf Association (USGA) The United States Golf Association (USGA) is the ruling body of golf in the United States and Mexico. They make the rules, decide which clubs and balls are legal for tournament play, and conduct all of the national championships of the United States, including the U.S. Open.

U.S. Amateur The national championship for amateurs in the United

Three-time U.S. Amateur winner Tiger Woods.

SAM GREENWOOD/PGA TOUR

States, the U.S. Amateur has been contested annually at match play (for most of its history). It was considered to be one of golf's four major championships at one point and, for the first thirty-five years or so of its existence, was considered more prestigious than the U.S. Open. Tiger Woods is a three-time winner of the U.S. Amateur.

U.S. Open The national championship of the United States, theoretically open to any contestant who wishes to attempt to qualify, is the U.S. Open. For its entire existence (since 1895 except during the two World Wars), it has been conducted at stroke play. It is considered one of golf's four major championships and is perhaps the most difficult of them all to win, being noted for its severely fast greens, narrow fairways, and deep rough.

U-turn This maneuver may be illegal in certain places while you're driving your car, but in golf it's just a big pain in the butt. When a putt seems destined to go in the hole—actually starts to drop in—and then spins out 360 degrees and starts to roll back toward you, that's a *U-turn*. And it ought to be a crime.

V

V The angles formed by your thumbs and forefingers when you grip the club are known as the *Vs* because of the resemblance these angles bear to the letter V. The location of these Vs is one way of determining the position of the hands on the club. In a neutral grip (see *neutral grip*), the Vs point to their respective shoulders.

Valley of Sin A large swale in the front of the eighteenth green at the Old Course (see *Old Course*), the *Valley of Sin* gathers in any shot played short into the green.

Harry Vardon's overlapping grip was eventually named for him.

Vardon grip An alternate term for the overlapping grip, in which a player places the right pinkie finger over the left index finger. The *Vardon grip* is named for Harry Vardon, the legendary English professional who won, among other things, six British Opens and the 1900 U.S. Open. Vardon is considered to be the first consistently masterful striker of the ball.

Vardon Trophy Also named for Harry Vardon, the Vardon Trophy is awarded annually to the PGA Tour player recording the lowest per round stroke average over the course of a season.

Vare Trophy The trophy awarded annually to the LPGA Player with the lowest per round scoring average for the year. Named for Glenna Collett Vare.

Vegas A betting game wherein the scores of partners are placed side by side, the lower numeral first, to form a single number. Points are awarded on the difference between the teams' numerals. For example, if you and your partner make a four and a six, and your opponents make a five and seven, you win eleven points (the difference between 46 and 57). This game is a quick way to win (or lose) a whole bunch of cash. If you and your partner both make birdie, your opponents must flop their numbers so that

Glenna Collett Vare, namesake of the Vare Trophy.

the higher goes first, i.e. the 57 becomes 75. Too bad for them, big bucks for you.

venue The course over which a tournament is played is sometimes referred to as the *venue* for that tournament.

V groove Traditionally, the grooves etched into the face of a club are shaped similar to the letter V.

vibration The shock that runs up the shaft of a golf club after impact is known as *vibration*. One of the perceived advantages of the graphite shaft is that it dampens vibration.

waggle Some players utilize a waggle to prevent the onset of tension before they begin their backswing and to rehearse their takeaway (see *takeaway*). The *waggle* is a loose movement of the clubhead back and forth behind the ball immediately preceding the takeaway. The *waggle* is usually made by flipping the wrists back and forth, although some players who are concentrating on making a one-piece takeaway (see *one-piece takeaway*) make a more stiff-armed waggle.

wagon Slang for a golf cart.

wake-up call A player can give himself a *wake-up call* or receive one from another player. If the player is cruising along in the lead of a tournament without anyone challenging then suddenly plays a bad hole or two, a commentator might say, "That should serve as a *wake-up call* for Jones," the inference being that if Jones keeps up his loose play, he'll blow his lead. Also, if Jones is a few shots ahead but Smith runs off a few birdies in a row to gain ground, the same commentator might say, "Smith is serving a *wake-up call* to Jones," the inference here being that if Jones thought he was in the clear, he had better think again.

Walker Cup A biennial competition between men's amateur teams repre-

Irishman Jody Fanagan was part of the combined Great Britain and Ireland team that defeated the United States at the 1995 Walker Cup.

senting the United States and Great Britain and Ireland (the latter two as a team).

walking bag A *walking bag* is any small golf bag, typically only large enough to hold the clubs and a few balls, which is light enough for the player to carry himself while he walks around the course.

walk with a match Golf fans who walk around following the progress of a match, no matter the level of competition, are said to be *walking with the match*. Even if you were at the Masters (where'd you get the tickets?) and decided to follow Tom Watson and Seve Ballesteros, it would be acceptable to say you walked with the Watson-Ballesteros match, even though they weren't actually playing a match.

waste area See *transition area.*

water ball Any old ball set aside by a player for use on holes with water hazards (just in case of an errant shot) is called a *water ball*. Using one is a public admission that you stink and you're cheap.

water club In the early days of golf, any of the countless clubs designed to be used to play shots from the water were called *water clubs*. The typical water club had holes or slots in it, the thought being that the water would pass through them. All clubs of this type are now banned.

water hazard Any body of water on a golf course that is marked as a hazard (typically with colored stakes in the ground) is a *water hazard*. If you hit your ball into one, it'll cost you two strokes. That is, unless you're nuts enough to play out of it (glub, glub).

watery grave What your ball goes to when you hit it in the water.

Watson, Tom The dominant player of the late 1970s and early 1980s, Watson has (as of this writing) won eight major championships including five British Opens. He is best remembered for two duels with Jack Nicklaus, both of which Watson won. The first was in the 1977 British Open when Watson fired 65-65 in the final two rounds to better Nicklaus's effort of 65-66. The second came in 1982 at the U.S. Open when Nicklaus birdied the third through seventh holes in the final round to shake up the field. Watson pitched in from beside the seventeenth green for birdie to secure the Open title.

wave up When you want the group behind you to hit to the green you're on, you *wave* them *up* with your arm. This is typically done on par-three holes, since some people believe this speeds up play.

waybacks The tees from which a course plays longest are sometimes called, among other things the *way-

Tom Watson after winning the 1977 British Open.

backs because you're way back from the green.

weak grip If your hands are turned excessively to the left on the club, you have a *weak grip* and probably hit a lot of slices as a result.

weapons A cool way to refer to your clubs is to call them your *weapons*. Also, next time you're curious about what type of clubs a player uses, ask him what kind of weapons he uses.

wedge *Wedge* can refer to either your pitching *wedge* or your sand *wedge* (see *pitching wedge* and *sand wedge*), but when you tell someone you hit a *wedge shot*, it means you hit a pitching wedge shot. If you hit a sand wedge, say so—don't call it a wedge.

what's it playing What you ask someone when you want to know the yardage of a given hole.

wheels fell off, the When you're playing well and suddenly start to play poorly, you might say *the wheels fell off*.

whiff In baseball, a swing and a miss (a strike) is sometimes referred to as a *whiff*. The term means the same in golf. However, if you whiff three times in golf, you're not out—but you should consider quitting for the day.

whins If you play golf in the British Isles, *whins* are natural vegetation just off the fairway, also known as gorse. The plants emit a natural magnetic field that attracts only golf balls and dodo birds. In the funniest golf book of all time, *The Dogged Victims of Inexorable Fate*, Dan Jenkins describes a scene at Turnberry when he asked his caddie if he was in the whins.

"Gorse is whin, right?" said Jenkins.

"Aye, the whins we call it," said the caddie. "You can'na plant the whin and neither will the whin die. The whin is just here where it always was."

I took a forceful swing with a sand iron, moving the ball about one foot, and said, "Don't forget to show me the heather when we find some."

"Aye," said the caddie. "That's heather you're in now."

whipping When woods were made of actual wood, *whipping* was the thin threading wrapped around the neck of the club where the clubhead and shaft were joined together. It helped to keep the clubhead from flying down the fairway after the ball.

whippy *Whippy* is a term used to describe the relative flexibility (see *flex*) of a shaft (see *shaft*). How much a club flexes when it's swung depends on how fast the player swings it. If a strong swinger swings a club with a shaft that has too much flex to it, he would describe the shaft as being *whippy*. The term refers to the feeling that the clubhead lags too far behind the hands in the downswing to achieve proper impact.

white paint When you're out on the course and you see *white paint* sprayed on the ground, the ground within the paint is ground under repair (see *ground under repair*).

white tees In the traditional coloring of tee markers, *white tees* are the men's tees at a golf course. To sound like a real golfer, just call them *the whites*.

Whitworth, Kathy One of the LPGA's all-time best players, Whitworth won 88 tour events, including six women's major championships. Her career spanned from 1959 to 1991.

Kathy Whitworth in 1969.

UPI/CORBIS-BETTMANN

wicket Slang for the flagstick, *wicket* is borrowed from croquet, which was a common pursuit at early country clubs.

windcheater A *windcheater* is a low, powerful shot played into a headwind, the idea being to keep the ball as close to the ground as possible where there is less wind. This is a good term to use if you happen to accidentally hit a low shot. "Just playing a little windcheater there," you can say with confidence. Just don't look at anyone when you say it. Of course, they'll know you're lying, but that's part of the game.

windmill hole A hole with a particularly poor design, a bit goofy even, is sometimes referred to as a *windmill hole*, a comparison to the most common type of hole on miniature golf courses (see *miniature golf*).

winter rules Because golfers can be numbered among the hardiest of souls, more immune to weather than even mailmen, they often head out of doors to pursue their beloved game in the wintertime. Golf courses generally go without maintenance in the wintertime—at least in regions where there is a true winter—and as a result, the ground can get a bit patchy as far as grass is concerned. In the interest of the winter golfer enjoying his game, some clubs enact a local rule called *winter rules*, which permits the player to improve his lie through the green. When such rules are in effect, the course usually posts a sign near the first tee that reads, "Play winter rules." Or, players can agree to play winter rules on their own.

wire-to-wire winner In multi-round stroke play events, a winner who leads the event at the completion of every round, first to last, is known as a *wire-to-wire winner*.

wolf This is a betting game that features a "wolf" on each hole, who is determined by the order of play from the first tee. For the sake of explaining this game, we'll call the players in your group A,B,C, and D and assume they play in that order from the first tee. Player A hits his tee shot, and if he decides he likes it, he can opt to play the hole on his own versus the other three players. His decision to go it alone is known as *wolfing it,* and it automatically doubles the bet for that hole. Under this scenario, if A wins the hole, he wins six points, two apiece from B,C, and D. If he loses the hole, he loses six points, two apiece to B,C, and D.

However, A doesn't need to play the hole alone. He can choose a partner. After B hits, A can choose him as a partner, but he must do so before C hits. Once C hits, A can no longer choose B. Now if A decides he wants C as his partner, he must declare that fact before D hits. If A does not choose C before D hits, A is stuck with D as partner. From that point on, the players play the hole at better ball for a possible point apiece (see *best ball*).

On the second hole, B hits first, and the same procedure follows. At the ninth and eighteenth holes, the player with the least amount of points plays first. At the tenth tee, the order returns to A,B,C, and D, no matter who held the tee at the ninth.

The fun part of this game is that you have different partners all day, but you're actually playing to increase your own point total.

wood The meaning of this term has changed somewhat over the years. Originally a *wood* was any clubhead made from wood. These clubs assumed a general shape over time, the clubhead having more mass to it than irons, with a broader sole and deeper club body in general. The greater mass of woods allowed players to hit the ball farther than they could with irons.

The game of golf changed, however, albeit at a slower pace than the world around it. Although metal clubheads in the shape of woods have been around since the 1930s, such clubs did not become popular among the masses until the mid-1980s. The modern metal wood proved so forgiving on mis-hit shots that it made actual wooden woods nearly extinct. And, for people with nothing better to think about, the new type of club created a question. Since woods took their name from the material from which they were constructed, should the metal versions of the clubs be called woods? Or should they be called metals?

As it turned out, the term *wood* had long ago ceased to refer to the material and came to refer to the shape of the clubhead. So metal *woods* are still called *woods*. Today, when you say *wood*, you can assume someone knows you mean a metal wood, without even bothering with the *metal* part. As for the folks who thought it a good idea to call metal woods *metals*, they can go back to worrying about jumbo shrimp, army intelligence, and other similar mysteries of the universe.

work the ball When a player has the ability to control the flight of the ball,

Fred Couples was legendary for his ability to work the ball.

SAM GREENWOOD/PGA TOUR

that is to say, he can draw it, fade it, hit it high, or hit it low—all intentionally and at will—he is said to be able to *work the ball*. And you should bow down before him.

Also, when a player predominantly hits a certain type of shot, for example, a fade, you would say he likes to *work the ball* from left to right.

wormburner A shot that sails along only inches from the ground for the length of its flight is a *wormburner*. You shouldn't take too much pride in such a shot, but at least by admitting to a *wormburner* you're displaying a sense of humor.

wound ball A three-piece ball is sometimes referred to as a *wound ball* because of the rubber bands that are wound around the core.

Wright, Mickey Considered the owner of one of the best golf swings of all time—for a man or woman— Mickey Wright ruled the LPGA Tour from 1955 through 1969, winning 54 events (55 total in her career) and twelve women's major championships.

Mickey Wright in 1959.

AP/WIDE WORLD PHOTOS

wrong ball Hit someone else's ball and you've played the *wrong ball*, which is a penalty. The good news: There's no penalty if you play the wrong ball in a hazard such as a bunker.

X What you put down as your score when you pick up on a hole (see *pick up*).

x-out A ball deemed by the manufacturer to be below its quality control standards has a bunch of Xs printed over its name and is sold for a heavily discounted price. Such balls are called *x-outs*.

Y

yank A putt that is pulled left of the hole is sometimes referred to as a *yank*. It's a good excuse to use in a disgusted tone of voice after a missed putt. "*Yanked* it," you can hiss as you slam your putter against your big toe.

yardage The term *yardage* can refer to the total distance a hole plays, a nine plays, or an entire course plays. Also, it can refer to the distance of individual shots as a hole is being played.

yardage book A little notebook in which a tour player's caddie or the player himself keeps track of the yardages for the course he is playing that week.

yardage marker A *yardage marker* is anything placed on a golf course that indicates the total yardage for a hole or the yardage from specific locations on a hole to the green. Some yardage markers have the precise distance posted on them while others, such as a distinct tree, indicate the approximate yardage to the green.

yips There is no precise definition for the *yips*, which are more a state of mind than anything else. The term refers to the frequent or complete inability of a player to control the putter on short putts—the hands twitch, the brain goes dark, the eyes glaze over, and the ball goes nowhere near the hole. All you need to know about the yips is that you don't want them. (See also *twitch*.)

You da man What drunk yahoos yell right after a tour player hits the ball.

Z

Zaharias, Babe Aside from being an Olympic gold medalist in multiple events in the 1932 Summer Games, Zaharias was a world-class golfer, winning thirty-one LPGA Tour events in a span of six years (1950 to 1956), including seventeen in 1955. Zaharias won three U.S. Women's Opens in that time span.

zone, the When everything is going right in your game and you're not even thinking about it, you're *in the zone*. Enjoy it while you can because you don't get many trips there.

Babe Zaharias in 1947.

UPI/CORBIS-BETTMANN